Shaland's Jewish Travel Guide to Malta and Corsica

Shaland's Jewish Travel Guide to Malta and Corsica

A Trusted Travel Companion
for the Jewish History Explorer

Irene Shaland

GTA BOOKS

 GTA BOOKS

Shaland's Jewish Travel Guide to Malta and Corsica

Copyright © 2021 by Irene Shaland

All rights reserved. No part of this book may be reproduced in any form by any electronic or mechanical means including photocopying, recording, or information storage and retrieval without permission in writing from the author.

Give feedback on the book at:
editor@globaltravelauthors.com

Cover by: Alex Shaland.

All photographs copyright © Alex Shaland
unless otherwise credited.
All rights reserved.

FIRST EDITION

ISBN: 978-1-7336245-4-1

Printed in U.S.A.

Dedication

To Alex: you are my love and my life. May we never know where one of us ends and another begins. Without your great talent as a writer and your inspiring support as an editor I would have never created anything.

This book is also dedicated to all those who lived through COVID-19 quarantines and lockdowns: may you all soon experience the delight of world travel and the excitement of adventures.

Contents

PART I

Malta: A Tiny Spot on the Map—a Linchpin of
World History   1

The Exploration of Malta Begins   4

The Maltese Prehistoric Period   14

The Phoenician Period in Malta and the First Maltese Jews 20

The Roman Domination and Early Christian Period   26

The Medieval Period in Malta and the Dissolution
of the Jewish Community   30

Exploring Jewish Sites of Medieval Malta   33

The Period of the Order of the Knights of Malta
and Jewish Slavery   41

Jews and the Inquisition in Malta   46

The Great Siege of Malta and the Jews   50

Giuseppe Cohen, the Most Remarkable Jewish
Personality in Malta during the Period of Slavery   53

The British Period (1800-1964) and the Rebirth of
the Jewish Community   58

Malta during World War II and the Safe Haven
during the Holocaust   61

The Maltese Jewish Community Today   64

PART II
A Field Guide to Exploration of Jewish History Sites
and Local Food in Malta   68

Finding Traces of Jewish Life during the Prehistoric
Period in Malta   73

Finding Traces of Jewish Life during the Phoenician
Period in Malta   75

Finding Traces of Jewish Life during the Roman and Early
Christian Period   78

Finding Traces of Jewish Life during the Medieval
Period in Malta   81

Finding Traces of Jewish Life during the Order
of the Knights of Malta Period   87

Finding Traces of Jewish Life during the British
Period in Malta (1800-1964)   94

Finding Traces of Jewish Life in Malta during World War II   95

The Maltese Jewish Community Today   97

Exploring Culinary Treasures of Malta   106

Select Movies Filmed in Malta   111

PART III
Corsica: The Island of Beauty, the Island of the Just   114

Corsica in Prehistoric Period   117

The Cradle of Corsican Independence   123

The Father of the Nation   126

Walking the Independence Trail in Corte   131

Corsica and the Jews	136
The Jews of Paoli	140
Ajaccio, Napoleon, and the Jews	145
Jews in Corsica in the 20th Century	151
Jews in Corsica during World War II	155
Back to the Question: What Made Corsicans—Corsicans?	159
Judaism is Alive and Well in Today's Corsica	161

PART IV
A Field Guide to Jewish History Sites and Local Food in Corsica — 164

Visiting Filitosa: the Most Famous Prehistoric Site in Corsica	166
Visiting Corte: the Cradle of Corsican Independence	170
Visiting Porto-Vecchio and the Levie Village: the Early Jewish Communities in Corsica	181
Visiting L'Île Rousse: the Jews of Paoli	183
Visiting Ajaccio: Napoleon and the Jews	186
Visiting Bastia: Home of the Only Synagogue in Corsica	194
Exploring Culinary Treasures of Corsica	197
Select Movies Filmed in Corsica	201
About the Author	203

Acknowledgments

This book would have never been written and published without my best friend and soulmate, first reader and editor, travel partner and photographer—my husband Alex. He inspired, encouraged, and supported me all the way, while his photographs beautifully illuminated the text.

My deepest gratitude goes to our new friends in Malta and Corsica who became vital contributors to this book.

In Corsica, Charles-Antoine Cesari, the Filitosa Prehistoric Site Director along with the members of the founder's family, and Maria Shelepova-Bartoli, the Education and Event Manager for the Site, were instrumental in helping us to understand the importance of the mysterious Statue-Menhirs and the island's strong ties to Sardinia. Charles' role in fact-checking and updating my Corsican part is truly invaluable.

In Malta, Joanne Grech Bianco, Historic Site Officer, Visitor Services and Events Manager for Heritage Malta, is a tour-guide par excellence, who guided us not only around the Maltese islands but also through multiple layers of this country's history. Joanne's insights and stories facilitated our understanding of Malta today and the archipelago's complicated history with its mysteries and contradictions. Joanne's fact-checking of my Maltese chapters and her assistance with getting several much-needed images proved instrumental for the story I intended to tell.

Sarah Azzopardi-Ljubibratic, Ph.D. in History of Religions and a co-founder of the Tayar Foundation for Jewish Heritage in Malta, who is widely regarded as an expert in Maltese Jewish history, provided unique insights through the Jewish history lens into the medieval and the Knights' periods. Sarah also facilitated my communications with the contemporary Jewish community of

Malta and its spiritual leader, Reuben Ohayon, whose story was indispensable for the completeness of my part about Malta.

I want to express my special thanks to Clive Cortis, an executive at Heritage Malta and a founder of Malta Private Guide Company, who connected me with Joanne and Sarah, and opened the doors to the Archival documents, Museums' collections, and historical sites that are normally closed to tourists. Without Clive's attention to my many requests, his knowledge of all things Malta, his business connections and organizational talent, my research objectives would not have been met. Thanks to Clive, we also met with Kenneth Cassar, Senior Curator of the Inquisitor's Palace and National Museum of Ethnography, and Sharon Sultana, Senior Curator of the National Museum of Archeology.

My warmest thanks go to both Ken and Sharon, who—to meet my research requests—guided us through the parts of their respective collections normally closed to visitors and then patiently continued to answer my emails filled with many questions. Clive also arranged our visit to the Cathedral Archives in Mdina, where we were able to see the collection of ancient Jewish documents going back to the 14th century. The (now late) Chief Archivist Sir John Azzopardi, Ph.D., an ordained priest and professor of Classical Greek and Religion, Prelate ad Honorem of His Holiness the Pope and Mr. Mario Gauci, Senior Assistant Archivist, serving as the Executive Research and Administrative Assistant to Sir John, set aside long hours from their busy schedules to share with us their unique knowledge of medieval Jewish life in Malta, and for that I am deeply grateful.

My special thanks go to the ANU Museum of the Jewish People in Israel (formerly known as Beit Hatfutsot). With permission from the late photographer-extraordinaire Louis Davidson and his wife Ronnie, the museum provided Davidson's beautiful images of the synagogue in Bastia. Louis Davidson dedicated many years of his career to documenting disappearing Jewish communities around the world and their houses of worship, often providing the last records of their existence. Louis Davidson passed away in September of 2020. May his memory be blessed.

My heart-felt gratitude goes to our dear friends and our daughter, who became devoted editors of this book, selflessly spending uncounted hours reading and re-reading my manuscript, offering their invaluable comments, and applying their editorial expertise and superb sense of the language to every chapter. Richard Holl, Sandra Kramer, Sophia Muchnik, Michelle Shaland, and Kelly Shepard, to you—passionate lovers of history and literature, you—my first readers, proofreaders, and editors, I owe an immeasurable debt of gratitude.

Both Alex and I are infinitely grateful to our friend and the final manuscript reader Corrine Joy Brown, an award-winning writer and *HaLapid* magazine editor, whose comments and suggestions became invaluable for the book completion.

Irene Shaland
August 2021. Cleveland Ohio.

PART I
Malta: A Tiny Spot on the Map—a Linchpin of World History

Why We Went to Malta

Malta's Jewish community today is small but flourishing and fully integrated into the prosperous, cosmopolitan, and inclusive society of this country. Maltese Jewish history encompasses thousands of years-old mysteries, literally etched in stone. It also incorporates glaring contradictions represented on one side by the nation deeply proud of its Knights of St. John's legacy and on another, by always-present dark memories of Jewish slavery during the Knights' rule.

View of the Fort of St. Angelo and the Great Harbor of Malta.

Indeed, the Jewish stories of Malta manifest a spellbinding trajectory still under-the-radar for most historians: from Israelites sailing there with Phoenicians three thousand years ago, to the first Jewish traveler, the Biblical Paul, arriving in Malta in the first century CE, through the dark times of slavery during the Knights of St. John's rule in the 16th century, to today's blossoming community. And, oh yes, here are a few facts for Jewish history enthusiasts: Malta has a fine kosher restaurant, observes Holocaust Remembrance Day, and was the only country to welcome Jews without visas during World War II. The Maltese language is Semitic in origin and is the only one of that kind that belongs to the twenty-four official languages of the European Union.

Malta's location in the Mediterranean.

The Maltese Archipelago.

The Malta archipelago is easy to overlook on the map: this tiny spot in the middle of the Mediterranean remains unknown to most U.S. travelers.

And this is a pity because if you do visit Malta, you will be forever inspired and spiritually enriched by the magical beauty of this gem that so far remains hidden for many. Do not be misled by Malta's size. This nation of fewer than half a million people embraces an astonishingly rich, millennia-old history that also includes a fascinating Jewish narrative. And all of it is crammed into three small islands: Malta, Gozo, and Comino. The Maltese culture is an amalgamation of influences from every major power through history: the Phoenicians, Carthaginians, Greeks, Romans, Byzantines, Arabs, Normans, Sicilians, Spanish, the Knights of St. John, the French, and the British.

I came to believe that it is imperative for the passionate and patient Jewish history buffs to "unpack" those influences while traveling through Malta's past and present.

The Exploration of Malta Begins

"Neither Jews nor rats can exist in Malta. The Maltese are too much for either." British Naval Admiral Lord Fisher, early 1900s. Quoted by Cecil Roth in his paper "The Jews of Malta read before the Jewish Historical Society of England," 1928.

I recited this quote to Joanne Bianco when she met Alex and me in the early morning of our very first day in Malta. Our new friend is a historian and researcher, and she stopped me right away: "But, Irene," she said, "Cecil Roth mentioned in his paper that the Admiral's knowledge of zoology (rats) was much better than that of history (Jews)." What the British historian and our friend wanted to point out was that the Jewish presence on Malta went back thousands of years, to "immemorial antiquity," as Joanne put it. And the best framework for understanding the Maltese Jewish story, according to Joanne, is ...well... Malta itself, in all its grandeur, complexity, and contradictions.

The Knights of St. John and the Unexpected Valletta

We chose the Maltese capital Valletta as our starting exploration point. The Knights of St. John (or the Knights of Malta) designed and built Valletta after their famous victory over the Turks in 1565.

Left: Exploring historic Valletta with Joanne.

Valletta street scene.

The Maltese claim that their capital is the first planned city in Europe. One of the many wonders of this country, Valletta is only one kilometer in length (or a bit over 0.6 miles) and 600 meters in width (just under 0.4 miles), and all its straight streets lead to the sea. Despite its small size, in 1980, Valletta was designated as a World Heritage site. Arguably, it is one of the most history-saturated areas in the world. Basking in its Baroque splendor, Valletta is also one of the most sophisticated micro-cities of Europe with its many drama and opera theaters, museums, art galleries, and Renzo Piano's cutting-edge architecture. However, the first things you notice in Malta are the balconies.

The first thing a visitor to Malta notices is the wooden balconies. These balconies could be of North African, Middle Eastern, or Sephardic origin.

The Balconies

Varying in size and color, but always wooden and always enclosed, these balconies are on almost every building you see in the old parts of the city. They are so ubiquitous all over the country, that they are often called Maltese in various guidebooks.

However, they are not of Maltese origin, as we learned from Joanne. It is possible that the design of the balconies was influenced by the Aragonese in the late 1400s. On the other hand, maybe that fashion began much later, in the 1700s, when two grand wooden balconies were added to the Grandmaster

The Grandmaster Palace in Valletta (1700s) with a majestic balcony called *galleria* by the Maltese.

Palace. The balconies, also called *muxrabija* (or the lookout place in Arabic) could be North African, Middle Eastern, or even Sephardic in origin. Balconies dating from the Knights of St. John period are called *galleria* by the Maltese.

During the rule of the Order, the Knights' preferred source of revenue was ransom they collected after attacking merchant ships and taking everyone onboard as captive slaves. From the mid-1500s until Napoleon got rid of the Order in 1798, Malta had numerous slaves working on the islands while waiting for their ransom to be

These *gallerias* might well be following the popular fashion introduced by the Grandmaster Palace.

paid. According to an expert on Maltese Jewish history, Sarah Azzopardi, in the 1600s there were at least 80 Jews among the slaves and even more in the late 1500s. Many of them were master craftsmen. They could have introduced these wooden balconies to Malta. In typical Maltese fashion, as we learned, there was often no single answer.

St. John's Co-Cathedral and Caravaggio

The Knights' presence is felt everywhere in Malta. One seems to breathe in the Baroque grandeur of the churches they designed, the power and strength projected by the amber-colored fortresses and bastions they constructed, and the ubiquitous Maltese Crosses they placed on building façades. Everything in this Maltese universe is surrounded by the turquoise waters of the Great Harbor and lit by the brightest sun one can imagine.

And the true crown jewel of it all is the resplendent St. John's Co-Cathedral in Valletta. St. John's is called a "co-cathedral" because, before the Knights' decisive victory over the Turks in 1565 and building of the new capital Valletta, there was already a cathedral in the old capital Mdina. While the cathedral in Mdina was dedicated to St. Paul, the new one in Valletta was named after the patron saint of the Order, St. John.

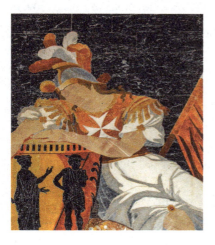

When in Malta, one sees Maltese crosses everywhere. This one, on a beautiful inlaid marble floor in St. John's Co-Cathedral, marks the burial place of a knight.

Valletta's cathedral is the main Roman Catholic Church in the country. It was financed by the Knights of the Order, designed by the Maltese architect Girolamo Cassar, and built between 1572 and 1577. The Cathedral's plain façade is in stark contrast with

Plain Baroque façade of the St. John's Co-Cathedral.

the overwhelming riches of the interior covered with gold leaf. It was created in the Baroque-Mannerist style by Mattia Preti, a Calabrian artist and a Knight of the Order. When we stepped inside the church, we clearly understood why this interior was considered among the finest examples of high Baroque architecture in Europe. It was extremely ornate, with intricately carved stone walls, a painted vaulted ceiling, and side altars. The figures from the scene of the life of St. John looked to us as three-dimensional statues, but that was a clever illusion created by the artist. Viewed as a whole, the entire marble floor of the Cathedral is a marvelous work of art. Underneath the floor there are tombs where over 400 knights are buried. The Grand Masters (heads of the Order) are buried in the crypt.

For us, the main treasure of the Cathedral was Caravaggio. Alex and I followed this great Italian artist looking for his masterpieces in museums and churches in Rome, Naples, Sicily, and now, in Malta where he lived and worked in 1607-1608. Why on earth did this supreme genius of the late Renaissance leave art centers like

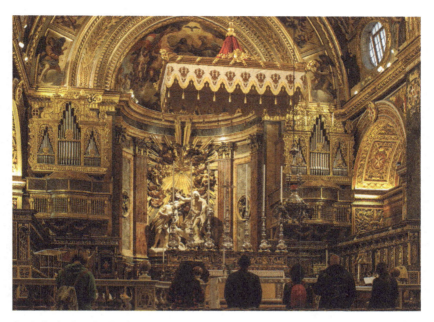

St. John's Co-Cathedral's gold-leaf interior was created in the Baroque-Mannerist style by Mattia Preti, a Calabrian artist and a Knight of the Order.

The entire marble floor of the Cathedral is a marvelous work of art. Over 400 knights were buried underneath marble tombstones. The Grand Masters were buried in the crypt.

Rome and Naples to arrive in Malta?

What could he hope to achieve living in the middle of the sea on this tiny rock occupied by soldier-monks (not exactly your usual art connoisseurs and patrons)?

Caravaggio was an archetypal artist-rebel. His turbulent life consisted of not only high art (like his unique *chiaroscuro* style) but also of high-drama: the never-ending succession of drunken brawls and fights. At the time of his arrival in Malta, he was a wanted fugitive on the run after killing a man in Rome. At the invitation of the Grand Master Alof de Wignacourt, Caravaggio became the official painter of the Order and even was given the title of the Knight of Magisterial Obedience in July of 1607. Not for long, however: in August of 1608, Caravaggio was arrested and imprisoned for wounding a high-ranking Knight. He managed to escape from his cell in the Fort of St. Angelo and was, of course, expelled from the Order.

But during his short tenure in Malta, Caravaggio created two masterpieces, *St. Jerome Writing* and *The Beheading of St. John the Baptist*. The *Beheading* is considered by the renowned expert in Baroque art, Andrea Pomella, to be "one of the most important works in Western painting." (A. Pomella, *Caravaggio: An Artist through Images*, 2005). We could not move away from that immense (12 by 17 feet) painting of human malice and brutal death depicted in bright blood-red and warm yellow colors. Red blood spilled from the cut throat of St. John to form the artist's signature, the only Caravaggio painting I know he signed.

The Cutting-Edge Architecture

"Now," announced Joanne, "I have to show you a Malta you did not expect." One of the greatest architects of our time, Renzo Piano is most known for his Centre Pompidou in Paris, the Airport Terminal in Osaka, the New York Times building, and the Whitney Museum of American Art (the latter two are both in New York City), just to name a few. He was working in Valletta, the last place in the world his aesthetics could be fitting, according to his many Maltese critics, from 2011 through 2015. However, what we saw seemed as integral to the Maltese capital as the sea, the sun, and the Maltese crosses.

Just take, for example, the Parliament Building: its ornamental stone façade seems to be conjuring Malta's heritage as a Mediterranean fortress, surrounded by nature-made cliffs and man-made bastions. From the time Valletta became Malta's capital in the 1570s until Renzo Piano's Parliament Building was completed in 2015, the country was ruled from the Grandmaster Palace located on the square right in the center of the city. That

The Parliament Buildings by Renzo Piano completed in 2015.

was never challenged, no matter who ruled Malta: the Knights of St. John, the French, or the British.

It took a ground-breaking architect to change that status quo. Piano's building is located at the entrance to the city, and this is where the Maltese parliament members now work: inside the 21st-century limestone box-like buildings that sit above the ground-floor entrance vestibules, behind their steel column porticoes. There are actually two buildings joined by a high-level steel bridge. This does not sound like a grand romantic description fitting Valletta's late Renaissance magnificence. However, when you closely look at the buildings' most striking feature, their stonework that gives them a strangely pierced appearance, the architecture does look to be naturally of Malta. The Parliament Buildings echo Maltese colors and textures and fit comfortably within that island, its history, and its Renaissance capital.

Renzo Piano's urban design plan comprises not only his parliament buildings but also incorporates the city walls, the city gates, and the remains of the Royal Opera House severely bombed by the Germans and Italians during World War II. That theater was designed in 1866 by Edward Middleton Barry, famous for his Royal Opera in Covent Garden, London. It was very British-looking: Malta was British until 1964. Instead of rebuilding the theater, Piano redesigned what was left of it in a poignantly poetic way making the theater look like ruins from romantic paintings of Hubert Robert or Caspar David Friedrich.

At the same time, Piano's parliament buildings looked to me more like museums or libraries rather than government structures. "This was intentional perhaps," remarked Joanne, "to illustrate the absence of hierarchies between the people and their elected government." Thanks to the genius of Renzo Piano, Valletta has become a modern 21st-century city. I was not a bit surprised when we were told that Valletta was called "The City" by the Maltese. In Maltese, "the City" is *Il-Belt*, and this is how Valletta is indicated on some road signs! Just as any New Yorker knows "the City" means only one place, Manhattan, and likewise, for the Maltese people, the City or *Il-Belt* is their unique capital.

Royal Opera House was severely bombed during World War II. Renzo Piano redesigned the ruins in a poignantly poetic way.

The Theaters of Malta

Redesigned by Piano, the Royal Opera is not by any means the only opera theater in Malta. This small nation enjoys at least four theaters dedicated entirely to opera and ballet, and one of these four is the oldest opera house in Europe: Teatro Manoel, 1731. That year, Antonio Manoel de Vilhena, the Grand Master of the Knights of Malta, authorized and personally funded the construction of what he called a public theater. Completed in just ten months, the theater was meant to keep the young Knights of the Order of St. John "out of mischief."

The Grand Master also wanted the theater to provide the rest of the population with "honest entertainment." Joanne pointed out that its motto reflected the Grand Master's objective: *ad honestam populi oblectationem*, or "the honest people's delight." The first performance, we learned, was a classic Italian tragedy, Scipione Maffei's "Merope." The Order's Chief Architect Francois Mondion designed the set, and the Knights were the actors.

Teatro Manoel in Valletta built in 1731 is the oldest opera house in Europe.

Travel through History
Searching for Jewish Stories

After we thoroughly walked through the Baroque Malta of the Knights and the "unexpected Malta" of Renzo Piano, Joanne said: "Now, if you want to find the Jewish stories of Malta, we need to travel through all layers of Maltese history." And thus our exploration of Malta set its course on discovery of the Jewish presence from the first known events to the Jewish community of today.

The Maltese Prehistoric Period

The mysterious prehistory of Malta is officially considered the period that began with the arrival of man in the islands and the appearance of the megalithic temples some time around 5200 BCE. It concluded with the colonization of Malta by the Phoenicians in approximately 800 BCE. You will find the megalithic temple-like complexes, massive, enigmatic, and strangely beautiful, all over the islands of Malta and Gozo. Claimed by archeologists to be the oldest free-standing structures on Earth, the temples are thought to be at least one thousand years older than the pyramids of Egypt. Definitely not defensive fortresses but most probably places of worship or gathering, they are considered by some researchers to

The megalithic temple-like complexes in Malta, like the one shown, are possibly the oldest free-standing structures on earth.

prove the theory suggesting that Malta was a "sacred island" where people would assemble for their mystic rituals. Even the name "Malta" is believed to have come from the Phoenician "refuge" or from Hebrew "escape." However, I also read that the word "Malta" might have come from the ancient Greek *melitos*, meaning honey. A typical multi-theory Maltese explanation, I thought, go figure.

Supposedly, the people who built these structures came from southeastern Sicily. What is evident is that they had developed a unique, non-militant, cultural society, in isolation and without any outside influences. Archeologists know that these prehistoric people traded with Sicily, but no evidence of any cultural exchange has been found. Their innovations were homegrown, developed in the process of their cultural evolution, and are unique to the Maltese Islands. Then, sometime after 2500 BCE, these innovators, artists, and builders disappeared.

To better understand the Maltese prehistoric mysteries we went underground, literally.

Visiting the Hypogeum

The word *hypogeum* indeed means "underground." The only structure of its kind in the world, this World Heritage Site is a masterpiece of prehistoric engineering: a maze of passages, corridors, rooms, temples, funerary halls, and cemetery, all dug out of the rock. Created somewhere between 5500 and 4500 years ago, the Hypogeum was a place of worship for the living and a burial place for their dead. The structure's underground architecture is well preserved over many millennia and is believed to mirror the building styles above the ground. Only a few guided tours are allowed daily, and each group cannot exceed ten people. I got our entrance tickets at least five months in advance. Walking these labyrinths was a mystical experience. What an extraordinary society it was, I thought, highly intelligent, artistic, resourceful, and peaceful.

Talking to the Heritage Malta historians (an organization similar to the Smithsonian Institution in the United States), we learned that, though a large body of contemporary scholarship exists, the

The author (right) and Heritage Malta historian, Joanne Grech (left), are getting ready to enter the Hypogeum.

particulars of the early Maltese islanders' life and traditions are veiled in mystery. However, multiple art pieces found in the Hypogeum and other temples dotting the archipelago are the evidence of their sophisticated lifestyle. This evidence is reflected in decorations of their structures and in clothing and hairstyles of their goddess-like female sculptures.

I was particularly enthralled by the Sleeping Lady found in one of the painted galleries in the Hypogeum and displayed in the Valletta Museum of Archeology.

Sleeping Lady was found in one of the galleries in the Hypogeum. Made of brown clay with traces of red, she is dressed in an elaborate long skirt and has an intricate hairdo. Photo courtesy of the National Museum of Archeology, Malta.

She is made of brown clay with traces of red ochre. Dressed in an elaborate long skirt, this reclining lady is a beautifully rendered little sculpture. Unlike the numerous earth-mother headless statues found across the islands, she has an intricate hair-do: was she a sleeping Mother-Goddess or a representation of Eternal Sleep?

Somehow, no male statutes were ever found. Perhaps theirs was a female-dominated society, where all women were regarded as goddesses. Clever people I thought.

Entering the World of Mystery in Ggantija Temple on the Island of Gozo

Our Valletta driver took us to the Cirkewwa port to board a ferry for a forty-minute crossing of the Gozo Channel to the island of Gozo. Gozo is small even by Maltese standards, and compared to Valletta, the island seemed to us quiet and laid back. An impressive massive Citadel built by the Knights dominates the capital city of Gozo. The Citadel dwarfs the city around it. Named Victoria, the capital has a population of about seven thousand people living within 1.1 square miles. Like many places in Malta, the capital has another name: it was called Rabat before the Knights of the Order of St. John's victory over the Turks in 1565. Today, both names

The capital city of Gozo, Victoria, is dominated by the massive Citadel.

The prehistoric Ggantija Temple in Gozo.

are used interchangeably, and not only to confuse the tourists! In Malta, the past is always present.

We knew that Gozo had its secrets, which waited for the students of Jewish history, to be discovered and pondered upon. We came to see the prehistoric Ggantija Temple not only for its immense size and uniquely decorated architecture but also for what was, until recently, considered as evidence of Jews living on the Malta archipelago at the time of the Phoenician colonization.

Ggantija, like all megalithic temples we explored, though different in plan, had the same internal rounded shape that reminded us of those headless mother-earth figurines we had seen in the National Museum of Archeology. Maltese temples have an elliptical court right in front of the concave façade. Walls often consist of upright stone slabs topped by horizontal blocks. The structures were reinforced by filling the inner chambers between the external and internal walls with stones and earth.

We learned that Ggantija, like other temples, most probably had corbelled arch-like roofs with horizontal beams on top, a remarkably sophisticated building solution invented by the early Maltese.

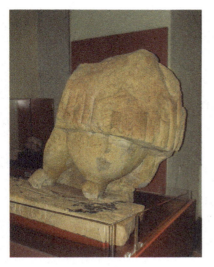

Ggantija was a perfect example for us to study the intricacies of prehistoric architecture. In addition, that temple had also allowed us to enter the world of mystery: arguably, the beginnings of the Jewish history on Malta and perhaps in the entire Mediterranean.

A "headless" earth-mother figurine. Photo courtesy of the National Museum of Archeology, Malta.

A "double portrait" from the Maltese prehistoric period. Photo courtesy of the National Museum of Archeology, Malta.

The Phoenician Period in Malta and the First Maltese Jews

Did the first Jews of Malta land in Gozo over three thousand years ago, and did they scratch their prayers on stones using the Phoenician alphabet? We needed Joanne's guidance to find the evidence of the ancient Jewish presence. It was right there, not far from the inner apse of Ggantija: the inscription in two lines and ten words, seven words in the first line and three in the second. When translated into English from what was Hebrew written in the Phoenician alphabet, this inscription reads: "To the love of our Father Jahwe" or in some sources, the translation reads "My father YHWH." The "YHWH" stands for Jahwe or the God of Israel.

The first image below shows the inscription the way you would see it when standing next to the stone wall. To make the characters more recognizable, we turned the image upside down, so that the characters appear right side up.

Ggantija's mystery. The stone-hard evidence of the ancient Jewish presence—or—a late forgery?

Translated into English from what was Hebrew written in the Phoenician alphabet, this inscription reads: "To the love of our Father Jahwe" or in some sources, the translation reads "My father YHWH."

Two British female explorers, N. Erichson and R. Cleveland, discovered that inscription in 1912 and made it known to historians and tourists alike. Though the authoritative study published by the Heritage Malta in 2013 stated that "there can be no doubts" that the inscription was genuine (*Ggantija: The Oldest Free Standing Building in the World*, 2013, page 17), the current position of the Heritage Malta, an acclaimed scientific authority on Maltese history, maintains that this inscription is a 19th-century forgery. Forgery or not, it is possible that the Jews did arrive in Malta with the Phoenicians. The Phoenician period of Maltese history spans the time from the beginning of their colonization of the archipelago in around 800 BCE until the year 218 BCE, when the Romans conquered Malta after their Punic Wars.

Under the Phoenicians, Malta passed from prehistory to history proper or recorded history. Where did the Jews fit into this record? Phoenicians were the first recorded group to colonize Malta. They were Semitic people, who lived along the coast of what is today Lebanon and Israel. They spoke a language similar to Hebrew and developed the first alphabet in the world. Unlike the cuneiform script of multiple pictorial symbols, the Phoenician invention used less than thirty letters, one for each sound, and was written like Hebrew, from right to left. Great maritime traders from the Persian Gulf, they settled many Mediterranean islands and established coastal cities like Mdina in Malta, Palermo in Sicily, and Nora in Sardinia, to name just a few.

The close relationship between the Phoenicians and the Jews could have started in the early 900s BCE with the marriage of Jezebel, daughter of the Phoenician Chieftain, to Ahab, King of Israel. Though considered an archetypal wicked woman according to the Biblical Book of Kings for instituting worship of pagan gods, Jezebel might have become an unwilling godmother of the Phoenician-Jewish partnership in sea exploration and marine trade. Various sources mention Jewish tribes like the prosperous Asher and seafaring Zebulun that sailed with the Phoenicians to Maltese islands. We have seen a few examples of a ship, the tribe of Zebulun's symbol, incised in the Jewish catacombs of Rabat and Tabja in Malta.

If indeed, as we learned, the ancient name of Gozo was Gaudos which may have meant "The Island of the Gadites," then it could as well be possible that another tribe of Israel, the one of Gad (meaning soldier or luck) was also among the first explorers joining Phoenicians in settling the islands of Gozo and Malta.

Perhaps it was Malta that influenced the change in the Phoenicians' original "business strategy." Traders as they were, Phoenicians had little interest in establishing stable colonies, but Malta, with its fine harbors and central location right in the middle of the Mediterranean, might have changed their mindset! It is thought that well before the Phoenicians' largest city Carthage was established (in what is now Tunisia), Malta with its aristocratic ruling class had already been well settled. Few remains of the Phoenician period survive throughout the Mediterranean. The only place where we saw a well-preserved remainder of the Phoenician walls was Palermo. However, archaeological findings and the astonishing collection of the Phoenician artifacts in the National Museum of Archeology confirm that even in the early years of the Phoenician colonization, Malta was home to a prosperous community.

After all, people should indeed be rich enough to build elaborate burials with chamber-tombs cut out of the rock, sumptuous sarcophagi, and various treasured items used for decorations.

This engraving of the seafaring Israelite tribe Zebulun symbol is found in the ancient Jewish burial inside the catacombs. Rabat, Malta.

The Phoenician Gifts: The Language and the Eye

The Phoenician invention of alphabetic writing spread across the world they colonized. The very word "alphabet" comes from "aleph" and "bet," the first two letters of the Phoenician writing system. By the first millennium BCE, the people of the Levant, like Arameans, Hebrews, and of course the Phoenicians themselves, were using a standardized alphabet, which was later transformed into other written languages such as Greek, Etruscan, and Latin. The Maltese, just like the Hebrews, were among the very first beneficiaries of that gift of literacy. Thanks to the Phoenicians and Hebrews that came with them, the Maltese language (called the Maltese or Malti) is Semitic.

The Language

The national language of the country, Maltese, is also one of the official languages of the European Union. It is the only Semitic language among the twenty-four EU official languages. To our ears, spoken Maltese sounded like a synthesis of Hebrew and Arabic. What we learned was that this language is indeed a Latinized form of medieval Arabic developed during the Arab domination in Sicily and Malta between 831 and 1091. When the Normans came at the end of the 11th century and began their process of re-Christianization of Malta, the language was gradually Latinized. As a result, any ties with what would have become classic Arabic were severed. Also, Maltese morphology has been deeply influenced by neighboring cultures and their Romance languages, Italian and Sicilian, and about half of the Maltese words come from those. Maltese is the only Semitic language written exclusively in the Latin script.

The Eye

When Joanne brought us to a fishing village called Marsaxlokk, it felt like we stepped inside a fairy tale. The turquoise waters were lit by the brightest sun we ever saw, and many fishing boats were anchored in the harbor, all painted in the brilliant colors of red, yellow, and blue. Every boat, no matter what the color, was painted reddish-brown or maroon on the lower half of the sides to mark the waterline. These boats are called the *mustacc* or *moustache* because the band above the lower half of the boat is shaped like one. If the mustacc is black that means there was a recent death in the family.

The fishing village Marsaxlokk with the brightly painted boats anchored in the harbor.

All boats have an eye painted on their prow.

All boats seemed to have a life of their own and they were staring at us, ogling us. All boats, without exception, had an eye painted on their prow. Did we find ourselves inside some otherworldly open-air art show? This "eye" is watching over the fishermen, explained Joanne, to protect them at sea. Another Phoenician legacy is alive and well in Malta after three thousand years.

The Roman Domination and Early Christian Period

The First Jewish "Tourist" Arrives

"I am Saul, a Jew, born in Tarsus of Cilicia... I was thoroughly trained in the law of our fathers and was just as zealous for God as any of you are today...." Acts 22:3.

The Greeks Hellenized Malta in the third century BCE. Then, the Romans conquered the archipelago in 218 BCE, and it remained a part of the Roman Empire until the early 6th century CE. We wanted to visit the ancient burial sites of that period, the catacombs at Rabat and Tabja, where the discovery of carved menorahs (candlesticks with seven branches) and Hellenistic inscriptions in several catacombs confirmed that a prosperous Jewish community existed in Malta in Grecian and Roman times.

St. Paul's Shipwreck Church, Valletta.

The first most renowned Jewish (by origin) visitor in Malta was the Biblical Paul who was shipwrecked on the Maltese coast in the year 60 CE. He persuaded the Roman Governor and most of the population to become Christians and is considered by the Maltese to be the spiritual father of the nation. Thanks to St. Paul, Malta today is one of the most pious of Catholic countries: they have

365 churches, and one can visit a different church every day of the year!

The Catacombs of Malta where Christians, Jews, and Pagans Are Buried Side-by-Side

We were driving toward the center of the island of Malta to visit the ancient catacombs or underground communal burials that date back millennia. Joanne reminded us that Malta has always served as a hub for all travelers between southern Europe and Africa, which inevitably led to a rich diversity of the population. Why should the Maltese dead be different? And the catacombs showed they weren't, revealing that Christians, Jews, and Pagans were peacefully buried there side-by-side.

I have mentioned earlier the city of Rabat located on the island of Gozo. However, there is also a Rabat on the island of Malta, which possesses one of the most important historical treasures—the St. Paul's Catacombs.

The Gates to the ancient city of Rabat.

This area is still known in Arabic as *tad-dlam* or "place of darkness." The archeologists began working on the site in the 19th century, but the locals had known for centuries of the burials deep underground. The catacombs of St. Paul and St. Agatha are the largest of all with a combined area of well over 22,000 square feet (or more than 2,000 square meters).

We went there to see the proof that Jews had been living in Malta during the Roman period. Slowly walking through the narrow passages cut in the rock carrying a flashlight, getting inside the burial chambers, and finding numerous menorahs chiseled in

Entrance to St. Paul's Catacombs, Rabat, Malta.

stone was a surreal experience. The three of us, Joanne, Alex, and I, were the only visitors at that time. Around us were burials where Jewish people were devotedly interred there by their loved ones over millennia ago. I wanted to let them know that they were not forgotten and left a small stone at the exit.

Inside St. Paul's Catacombs, Rabat, Malta.

A menorah marks a Jewish burial inside St. Paul's Catacombs.

The Medieval Period in Malta and the Dissolution of the Jewish Community

After the Romans, Malta fell under Byzantine rule, and then in 870 CE, was captured by the Arabs. And this is when the medieval period in Malta began. Then, the Normans (north of France) came in 1090, followed by the Swabians (now Bavaria, Germany) in 1194, the Angevins (French royal house) in 1266. In 1479, the Aragonese established Spanish rule. The medieval period in Malta ended in 1530, when Carlos the Fifth, the King of Spain and the Holy Roman Emperor, gifted Malta to the Knights of St. John.

During the Arab rule, Jews were treated with respect as People of the Book, and they often held posts as civil servants, sometimes even reaching the rank of a Vizier, the highest possible administrative officer. According to several authoritative studies, like Cecil Roth's *Jews of Malta* (Society, 1918) and Godfrey Wettinger's *The Jews of Malta in the Middle Ages* (Midsea Books, 1985), the Jewish population grew further under the Normans and Swabians to five hundred or so inhabitants. There were about 25 large extended families on the island of Malta and eight families in Gozo. At that time, Jews comprised close to one-third of the entire population in the Maltese main city Mdina.

In 1492, the infamous Edict of Expulsion became the law in all the lands under the Spanish crown, including Sicily, Sardinia, and Malta. Administratively, the Malta archipelago became a part of the Kingdom of Sicily in the 11th century and therefore it fell under the Spanish rule. Malta became subject to all the laws that existed in most of Italy south of Naples. Just as was the case with Sicilian Jewry, in Malta too, local authorities pleaded with the "most Catholic Monarchs" (Ferdinand of Aragon and Isabella of

Castile) to reconsider their Edict of Expulsion. The Edict, the authorities feared, would lead to a collapse of the economy and depopulation. However, the Spanish came up with an ingenious solution: they forced the Jews to pay compensation for the loss of tributes caused by ... their departure. Each person was allowed to take only one set of common clothing, a mattress, a pair of worn shoes, and a little bit of food for the journey.

Some Jews who left Malta went first to Sicily, then up to the north of Italy, but some came to the parts of the world dominated by the Ottoman Empire that was benevolent to Jews, such as Greece or Turkey. Those who stayed had to convert to Catholicism and...disappear into Malta. What is left from the blossoming and rich community in Malta are the names: those of the streets and the conversos, such as surnames common in today's Malta like Elul (a month in the Jewish calendar) or Azzopardi (Sephardi Jew). I do need to note here that some Jewish historians in Malta, like Sarah Azzopardi for example, are cautious when speaking about the Maltese surnames that might have Jewish origins since there are no direct sources to support the connection. It is tempting to imagine, however, that all Azzopardis or Eluls have Jewish ancestry!

The Most Remarkable Jewish Figure in Medieval Malta and the Island of Comino

Joanne called our attention to the island of Comino when we passed it by while sailing from Malta to Gozo. Called Ephaestia by the Greeks, this tiny island of just 1.4 square miles (or 3.5 square kilometers) is located between the islands of Malta and Gozo. The Romans who settled on Comino were farmers and most probably gave the island its name after the herb cumin that used to be abundant there.

The island's coastline consists of vertical limestone cliffs, and, as Joanne told us, also has many deep caves, which were popular with pirates. The pirates used those caves for hiding before attacking helpless boats crossing the waters between Malta and Gozo. Currently, the total population of Comino consists of three people, after the fourth one passed away a few years ago.

View of the island of Comino from the ferry.

However, this tiny island has an illustrious place in Jewish history because of one Jewish sage who lived there from 1285 until 1291.

His name was Avraham Abulafia (1240-1291). A visionary philosopher far ahead of his time, Abulafia founded the school of "Prophetic Kabbalah" and dreamed of dissolving the differences between Judaism, Christianity, and Islam. He wrote two books: *Sefer Ha-ot* (or *Book of the Signs*) and *Imre Sefer* (or *Goodly Works*) that were famous in medieval Judaism. An eccentric man, Abulafia proclaimed himself the Messiah and predicted that the messianic era would begin in 1290.

He believed he would be able to persuade the Pope to support close relationships between all three Abrahamic religions and convince him to stop persecuting the Jews. So, he went to Rome and requested an audience with Pope Nicholas III. Alas, the pope instead accused Abulafia of heresy and sentenced the Jewish philosopher to death by fire. Then, the Pope died of a heart attack; everyone thought it was a sign from God, so the philosopher was released. Abulafia went to the Maltese island of Comino where he passed away in 1291 at the age of 51.

Exploring Jewish Sites of Medieval Malta

Jews in Medieval Gozo

While exploring the ancient capital city of Gozo, Joanne brought us to what is believed to be a pre-Expulsion Jewish Quarter.

Jewish Quarter in Gozo's capital Victoria.

The street sign Triq IL-Fosos indicates the area where the Jewish Quarter in Gozo is believed to have been located.

The street named Triq IL Fosos (the Ditch Street) along the north side of the Cathedral led us into the area of narrow medieval streets and ancient buildings. A plaque on the wall explained that this was a location of the Jewish Quarter in medieval times.

In the year 1240, Gilberto Abbato reported to his master, Swabian King and Holy Roman Emperor Frederick II, that there were a total of 1119 families living in the Malta archipelago at that time. Among them, Jews constituted 33 large families, including eight families living in Gozo. (Cecil Roth's *Jews of Malta,* 1918 and Godfrey Wettinger's *The Jews of Malta in the Middle Ages,* 1985).

This tiny Gozo community played an important, disproportionate to its size, role in the island's economy. The Jews of Gozo paid taxes to the City

University and held a monopoly as apothecaries and dyers. Today, neither the location of the synagogue nor that of the local Jewish cemetery is known. All that is left from that small hard-working and prosperous community is the memory of where they used to live centuries ago, indicated by the plaque on the building wall near the Cathedral. We stood there for a while imagining a bustling Jewish neighborhood that, along with its inhabitants, was destroyed after the Edict.

Mdina—The Ancient Capital of Malta, the Center of Jewish Life in the Archipelago

In the Phoenician period, the most important city in Malta was the very first one they established and called Maleth. When Malta was captured by the Arabs, the capital city was renamed Mdina, and the name stayed. The Knights of St. John came to Malta in 1530, and they used Mdina as their central city until they built Valletta, which became the capital in the 1570s.

Mdina was significantly damaged during the 1693 earthquake and was rebuilt in Baroque style. The cathedral was designed by the Maltese architect Lorenzo Gafa. A French architect Francois

View of Mdina.

Location of the ancient Jewish Quarter in Mdina.

de Mondion built the magisterial palace. Though not a capital anymore, Mdina is still impressive today dominating the center of the island. Despite the Baroque makeover, the walled city of Mdina managed to preserve its medieval character. Perhaps this is why Mdina's narrow alleys and piazzas with elegant palazzos served as the setting for the first season of *Game of Thrones*.

Stepping through the gates of Mdina and walking its centuries-old streets, we remembered that during the medieval period, one-third of that ancient capital's population was Jewish.

A sign marks the old Jewish silk market on Carmel Street.

A sign marks the old Jewish silk market on Carmel Street.

Within the walls of Mdina and elsewhere in Malta, Jews lived side-by-side with Christians.

Joanne brought us to the old Jewish Quarter. It was never a ghetto locked from outside. The Silk Market and the synagogue were the centers of Mdina's Jewish life. However, the Jews were required to wear red pieces of cloth to ensure people knew who was a Jew, and the men had to shave their beards. Jews were very important for the island's economy in general and their services to the city in particular. In Mdina for example, Jews were exempt from guard duty because they supplied oil for the street lamps.

Viewing Ancient Jewish Documents in the Mdina Cathedral Archives

During our short time in Malta, we would not even dream of the possibility of seeing ancient documents related to the medieval period of Jewish Maltese history. However, our good friend Clive Cortis did. The founder and owner of the Malta Private Guide Company and a historian himself, Clive understood my mindset very well. Even without knowledge of the language, just to observe the period documents and talk to expert archivists would provide a priceless opportunity for a researcher. An executive at Heritage Malta, Clive opened doors for us to the archival and museum collections and to some historic sites that would otherwise be closed to outsiders.

At the Mdina Metropolitan Cathedral Archives, we were met by the Chief Archivist Sir John (or Monsignor Dun Gwann) Azzopardi, Ph.D. and Mr. Mario Gauci, Senior Assistant Archivist, serving as the Executive Research and Administrative Assistant to

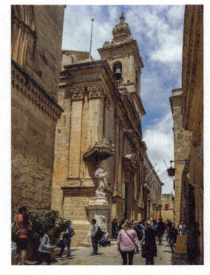

Walking toward the Mdina Cathedral.

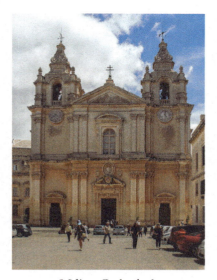

Mdina Cathedral.

Late Sir John Azzopardi, Ph.D., (1937-2021).

Dun Gwann. Dr. Azzopardi, an ordained priest and professor of Classical Greek and Religion, was also Prelate ad Honorem of His Holiness the Pope and Chaplain Grand Cross of the Sovereign Military Order of St. John.

Mr. Mario Gauci, Senior Assistant Archivist, showing the author research documents related to the ancient Jewish history in Malta.

Documents from the archival collections related to Jewish history on the islands. Photo used with permission by Mdina Cathedral Archives.

This oldest surviving document from the Archives collection dated 1342. Photo used with permission by Mdina Cathedral Archives.

A medieval Jewish notarial manuscript written in colloquial Maltese using Hebrew alphabet. Photo used with permission by Mdina Cathedral Archives.

Dr. Azzopardi was also a renowned historian who published and edited several books and catalogs on the Pauline (St. Paul's) cult in Malta as well as on art, music, and history. Likewise, Mr. Gauci distinguished himself as a participant in, and contributor to, several international conferences and publications.
(Note: Mr. Azzopardi passed away in February 2021).

Our illustrious hosts had prepared several documents from the archival collections related to Jewish history on the islands. The oldest document was dated 1342 when Jews constituted over thirty percent of the Mdina population. The medieval Jewish notarial manuscripts, including those we saw, were written in colloquial Maltese but using the Hebrew alphabet.

The majority of the documents referred to trade, loans, and payments. In the post-Expulsion papers, like records from the Town Council, we were able to see lists of new conversos. Many of the Jews whose business and legal matters were mentioned in the archival documents were still here, we were told, lying in eternal peace at the Kalkara cemetery. And that was where we headed, continuing our exploration of Maltese Jewish history.

The Kalkara Cemetery

As we learned from our esteemed hosts in the Cathedral Archives, the oldest existing reference to the ancient Jewish cemetery in Malta goes back to the late 14th century. At that time, the Aragonese Kings of Malta and Sicily granted the *Universitate Judeorum*, or the Jewish community, a plot of land to use as a burial place. Though no medieval Jewish cemeteries exist in Malta today, we were advised to visit the oldest existing cemetery, Kalkara, established in the 1700s.

Entering the Kalkara Cemetery, the oldest existing Jewish cemetery in Malta.

The oldest grave in the Kalkara cemetery.

The cemetery is closed to the public today, but thanks to our friend Clive Cortis, a representative of the Jewish community of Malta opened the ancient doors to the site for us. We walked along the overgrown paths in between ancient burials leaving small stones on some graves.

When we exited, Joanne pointed out the plaque on the wall dated to the Knights' period. It was the Knights' authorization for the cemetery, the copy of which is preserved at the National Library of Malta. Translated from Latin into English, the sign proclaimed: "This cemetery was established by the Leghorn Fund for Ransoming Hebrew Slaves, at its own expense, for the burial

The author and Joanne walking along the overgrown paths in between centuries-old burials.

The plaque on the wall of the Kalkara Cemetery.

of the dead of the race." What? Hebrew slaves?!

"Yes," confirmed Joanne, "Under the Knights of St. John, Malta became the last European stronghold of slave trading and slavery, until the Knights capitulated to Napoleon in 1798." Furthermore, over eighty percent of slaves in Malta were Jews and Turks.

To learn more about that historic phenomenon of Jewish slavery, we needed to explore, or as Joanne put it, "walk through" the period of the Knights of Malta.

The Period of the Order of the Knights of Malta and Jewish Slavery

Avadim hayinu le-parashim be-Malta ("We were horsemen's slaves in Malta"), from the 17th-century Passover Haggadah, Venice. Quoted in Derek Davis' essay "Jews before the Malta Inquisition," 2016.

The Knights of St. John of Jerusalem, Cyprus, and Rhodes arrived in Malta in 1530 after they had been driven from the Greek island of Rhodes by the Turks, and the Holy Roman Emperor Carlos the Fifth of Spain granted them the Maltese islands as a base. By the Emperor's decree, the Knights replaced the House of Aragon as the ruler of Malta. All they had to pay for the gift was an annual present of one white Maltese falcon to the King of Spain and another one to the Spanish Crown's Viceroy of Sicily. That low-cost rent came with strings attached. The Emperor ordered the Knights to fortify the islands and make Malta an impenetrable European defense post against the Ottoman Turks. The Knights' rule lasted until Napoleon conquered Malta in 1798 en route to Egypt. He outlawed slavery and banished the Order from the islands. But who were those Knights?

When founded in 1090, the original name of the Order was the Knights of the Hospital of St. John in Jerusalem. Taking care of the sick, pilgrims and Crusaders alike, the Knights became famous all over Europe for their bravery in battle and their medical skills. For example, they were the first to recognize the importance of cleanliness, separation of the very sick from the rest, and the usage of silver as an antibacterial material. Though the antibacterial properties of silver would not be scientifically proven for a long time, the Knights however, did use only silver utensils in their hospitals.

The Grandmaster Palace of the Order of the Knights of St. John of Jerusalem, Cyprus, Rhodes, and Malta.

Right: Authentic Knights' armor from the Order's collection. The Grandmaster Palace, Valletta.

When Jerusalem was lost to the Muslims in 1291, the Knights withdrew to Cyprus, but in less than twenty years, they were defeated by the enemy and had to retreat to the island of Rhodes in 1310. They stayed in Rhodes until 1530 when after losing to the Turks the Knights had, once again, to evacuate. The Emperor came to the rescue with his gift of Malta but with the strict order to the Knights to turn Malta into the most secure Christian shield against the Ottoman Turks. And they did. There are no forests in Malta today: all trees were cut down to build fortifications and for other defensive construction projects and, no less importantly, to provide good visibility of who is approaching the islands from the sea.

Since the Knights were technically not Hospitaller anymore, the only reason for their existence was the continuing state of hostility between the Christian and Muslim worlds. The Knights waged never ending maritime warfare, often not distinguishable from piracy. They captured vessels, brought them to Malta, and sold the entire crew and passengers into slavery. The captives were anyone who happened to be sailing on the unlucky ship. The Knights did not target Jews as Jews, but Jews made up a large part of the merchant class, and a high number of them were on many vessels sailing the Mediterranean. When the Knights raided Muslim seaports and carried off their inhabitants into slavery, Jews formed a considerable element in the captured population. These prisoners were taken back to Malta and held until ransom could be negotiated and raised.

Jewish Slavery in Malta, 16th-18th Century

Since the mid-1500s, the islands of Malta had become for the Jews a symbol of all that was cruel and hateful in the hostile world. The name Malta in Jewish literature was often associated with evil. I found a reference to a messianic prophecy from the 1600s, which predicted the fall of the four ungodly kingdoms, with the first of them being Malta.

Neither piracy nor ransom for captives was news in the medieval world. However, since the *corso del mare* piracy became a popular sport for the Knights, and the ransom money turned into their preferred source of income, there was a continuous flow of Jewish captives to Malta. The Jewish world had to react swiftly and establish a permanent organization to deal with the "new permanent" situation. The Jewish Society for the Redemption of Captives or *Hebrath Pidyon Shvuyim* was founded in Venice and Amsterdam. Donating to the Redemption of Captives was considered among the highest priorities of charity in the Sephardic world. When a dying Jew left his money "for the performance of

The Jews' Sallyport. Free Jews could only enter and leave through the gates still known today as the Jews' Sallyport.

good deeds" without any specifics, the money was directed straight to the *Pidyon Shvuyim*.

The main channels for freeing the Maltese Jewish slaves were the Jewish communities in Venice and Amsterdam. In addition, other communities all over Europe began collecting ransom money in a highly organized manner. For example, as mentioned in the "Jews before the Malta Inquisition" essay by D. Davis, Sir Moses Montefiore in 1895 was shown a ransom remittance for Malta Jewish captives sent from London's renowned Bevis Marks Synagogue. Sir Montefiore was quite impressed and noted the episode in his diary.

In Malta, the *Pidyon Shvuyim* maintained a resident agent whose sole responsibility was to bargain and make payments to the Knights. That agent was known as the *Procuratore degli Ebrei* or the Jews' Consul.

However, the Knights, apparently believing that all Jews were rich and miserly, practiced extortion, holding out for years and years to obtain the highest possible ransom. That led to a strange phenomenon described by Godfrey Wettinger in his book *The Jews of Malta in the late Middle Ages*, Periodicals Service Co., 1985. From 1492, the year of the Edict of Expulsion, until the year of 1798 when Napoleon banished the Order from Malta and proclaimed human rights and freedom to the Jews, the Jewish population of the archipelago was almost exclusively made up of Jewish slaves. Free Jews who came to Malta, often to conduct ransom negotiations, had to seek permission from the Grand Master of the Order and could only enter and leave through what is still known today as the Jews' Sallyport.

The Slaves' Prison Building

At the beginning of the Knights' hunting-for-captives strategy, all slaves were kept in a slaves' prison in the original Knights' headquarters in the town of Birgu. But soon, a much larger facility was required and built in Valletta. All captives, including Jews, were allowed to work, practice their craftsmanship and earn money, but they had to return to the prison at night. The original structure in Valletta was destroyed by the German and Italian air raids during World War II. What we could see while visiting the site was a memorial plaque on a modern apartment building.

The site of the slaves' prison.

Jews and the Inquisition in Malta

Our new friend Sarah Azzopardi-Ljubibratic, Ph.D., was instrumental in helping us to understand the inner workings of the Maltese Inquisition and its unique attitude towards the Jews. With Joanne's and Clive's introductions, we first met with Sarah for lunch in the popular Café Cordina.

A one-minute walk from the Grandmaster Palace, this Valletta icon has the best food and service, but is the worst place ever for a conversation. Nevertheless, despite deafening crowd noise, we could not stop talking!

Ours was a true meeting of the minds; we had so much to share. A Swiss woman from Lausanne, Sarah wrote her doctoral dissertation on the subject of the Jews in Malta and the Inquisition.

She married a Maltese man and made her home in Valletta, where she is widely regarded as an authority on the Jewish history of the island. For the overwhelmingly Catholic population of Malta, Jews in their history and those in their midst today remain a mystery.

Learning from Sarah Azzopardi, Ph.D. about the Inquisition in Malta.

Although there are many Maltese families with names such as Elul or Azzopardi that suggest a Jewish origin (including the Chief Archivist of the Mdina Cathedral and Sarah's husband) that connection remains often unknown to its bearers. And so it happened that, in a Maltese extraordinary way, a young non-Jewish woman from Switzerland came to Malta to work on her thesis about the Jews in a period of slavery, married a local man with

The Inquisition Tribunal in the Inquisitor's Palace, now the National Museum of Ethnography.

a surname Azzopardi, and became a recognized authority on the subject.

Though indeed after the Expulsion, the Jewish community in Malta was practically entirely made of the slaves of the Knights, Sarah's research uncovered the existence of an embryonic community of crypto-Jews within the larger group of Jewish slaves in the Maltese archipelago. Those were the Jews who converted to Christianity but secretly practiced their former religion. Sarah called them the people with "a double identity: externally Christian, but internally Jewish." She also mentioned that contacts between neophytes (or new Christians, Jews who recently converted to Christianity) and Jews, whether slaves or free, were forbidden. However, some sources claim that those contacts existed anyway. Moreover, Jews who remained true to their religion might have encouraged some neophytes to secretly preserve their Jewish practices.

However, some Jews decided to stay in Malta, convert to Catholicism, and stop practicing their old religion even in secret.

Inside the torture chamber. The Inquisitor's Palace, now the National Museum of Ethnography.

According to Sarah, there is evidence showing that these three sectors, two tiny ones like crypto-Jews (neophytes who followed Judaism in secret), the non-Judaizing neophytes, and a very large group of the enslaved Jews—were all in contact with each other. These three Jewish sectors, of which is safe to say, an entire Jewish community in the archipelago at the time, were under the jurisdiction of the Inquisition.

The Inquisition Office was established in Malta in 1561. The original records of the Maltese Court of Inquisition covering the period between 1580 and 1792 are located in the Cathedral Archives in Mdina. As we learned from Dr. Azzopardi and Mario Gauci while visiting the Archives, only around one hundred cases involved Jewish defendants from among the slave prisoners. Those Jews were charged not with Judaizing but with such offenses as blasphemy. Remember, this was the Roman Inquisition, which, unlike the Spanish one, seldom sentenced prisoners to death. During its existence in Malta, no more than seven death sentences total were documented.

Each of the accused had to be summoned to verify the accusation, thus witnesses played an important role in the Inquisition-led investigations. The Inquisitor could summon anyone to testify. For example, the great artist Caravaggio received an "invitation" in 1607. Instead of the auto-da-fe burnings, the Roman Inquisition in Malta practiced a sort of a propaganda campaign. When we visited the Inquisitor's Palace in Vittoriosa, now the National Museum of Ethnography, we had a chance to see a curious treatise from the Palace collection. As a seventeenth-century "call to action," the treatise instructed Christians to actively engage in convincing Jews and Muslims to convert to Christianity.

The Great Siege of Malta and the Jews

"Nothing is better known than the siege of Malta."
Voltaire.

It is impossible to spend even a day in Valletta and not to come across numerous references to the pivotal event in the Maltese (and entire European) history: the Great Siege of Malta of 1565. Even now, more than five centuries after the Siege, it is commemorated annually with a series of events encompassing exhibits, concerts, processions, and liturgical church celebrations in memory of the fallen. Members of the Order of Malta come to the event to take part in the festivities. And there is a good reason behind this centuries-long collective memory. In the spring of 1565, the Ottoman Empire with an overwhelming force tried to invade the islands of Malta. The Knights under the command of the Grand Master Jean Parisot de Valette, with approximately 2,000 foot soldiers and 400 Maltese men, women and children, withstood the siege and repelled the invaders.

The Great Siege of Malta that concluded with the Knights' spectacular victory over the Ottomans became one of the most celebrated events in sixteenth-century Europe. The Siege was the climax of an escalating war between the Christian alliance and the Islamic Ottoman Empire for control of the Mediterranean. Historians believe that the Knights' illustrious triumph had led to the wearing away of the European perception of Ottoman invincibility. It also assured the Spanish domination of the Mediterranean.

Following the victory, the new capital Valletta named after the celebrated Grand Master was designed and built. In addition, the fortified town of Birgu located on the south side of the Grand Harbor was renamed Citta Vittoriosa (or "Victorious City") to commemorate its vital role in the defeat of the Ottomans. As it often happens in Malta, both names Birgu/Vittoriosa are used today—the practice that adds its share to a visitor's confusion!

For the captive Jews, the Knights' victory meant that their prison in Birgu was transferred to a larger building in the new capital city. Also, despite the circulated rumors that the Turks were partially financed by Jewish money, Jewish heroism during the Siege had become well known. For example, many Jews chose to join the relief expedition to liberate Fort St. Elmo, though such a mission might have ended in death. Claire-Eliane Engel, a historian, remarked that "the Jews of Malta behaved with loyalty above all praise." However, loyal or not, they still remained enslaved.

A fresco depicting events during the Great Siege of Malta. The Grandmaster Palace. Photo courtesy of Heritage Malta.

The main square in Birgu, the city that played a key role during the Great Siege of Malta in 1565.

A beautiful marina in Birgu. The city was renamed Citta Vittoriosa (or "Victorious City") to commemorate its vital role in the defeat of the Ottomans.

Giuseppe Cohen, the Most Remarkable Jewish Personality in Malta during the Period of Slavery

Clive Cortis once again was instrumental in our research about an important Jewish personality in the history of Malta. He arranged for us to meet with expert curators at the National Museum of Ethnography and the National Museum of Archeology. There, we were given a unique opportunity to see special collections, not accessible to the general public. The man we were after was Giuseppe or Joseph Cohen. In 1749, he was credited with nothing less than saving Malta from the Turks and by extension, changing the tide of European history.

Cohen was a Jewish slave who worked in a tavern in Valletta. One day, he overheard Muslim slaves conspiring against the Knights. As historical narrative has it, the Muslim revolt was to start with food poisoning at the Grand Master's banquet given in honor of the Feasts of St. Peter and St. Paul. The rebel's plan was to murder the Grand Master Manuel Pinto de Forseca himself, overpower his guards, free Muslim slaves from the prison, and finally attack Fort St. Elmo and capture its weapons arsenal. The Ottoman fleet was then to come from Tunis and Algiers to invade Malta upon receiving the signal from the rebels.

There was nothing strange about slaves gathering at a tavern at their leisure. At that time, there were around 9,000 Muslim slaves in Malta. While waiting for their ransom to be negotiated and paid, the slaves were given a substantial degree of freedom to work and to assemble for prayers or otherwise. Although laws forbade slaves to mix with the locals, these laws were not enforced.

Cohen, who knew multiple languages, understood and memorized all the details. Then, with great difficulties and dangers for a slave, he managed to gain an audience with the Grand Master and told him about the plot and the specifics he overheard.

Thanks to Cohen's brave intervention, the plot was uncovered and the conspirators arrested, interrogated, tried, and executed. If the rebels had succeeded, the Turks would have captured Malta, the key to the entire Mediterranean and to Europe. European and world history might have had a very different narrative.

The author and Joanne on the way to the Inquisitor's Palace in Vittoriosa.

Cohen Story Continues at the National Museum of Ethnography, the Inquisitor's Palace

To learn more about Cohen and the events of 1749, we headed to the Inquisitor's Palace, now the Museum of Ethnography, where we met with its Chief Curator, Kenneth Cassar. After giving us an excellent tour of the Inquisitor's Palace and the explanation of the Inquisition practices in Malta, Ken took us to a secure room where a not-yet-exhibited collection was held in the process of restoration.

The collection, gifted to the Museum by a prominent donor, consisted of 19 never-before-seen colored drawings that depicted in detail the story of the plot: Cohen coming to the Grand Master, the interrogations of the conspirators, the trial, and the executions including the depiction of severed heads displayed on the city walls.

The author with Dr. Kenneth Cassar, the Chief Curator of the National Museum of Ethnography (formerly the Inquisitor's Palace).

Giuseppe Cohen, a Jewish slave in Valletta, is reporting to the Grand Master Manuel Pinto de Forseca the details of the Muslim plot in 1749. From the Museum's collection of the 19 period drawings that depicted the story of the plot. Circa 1749. Courtesy of the National Museum of Ethnography, Malta.

As Kenneth Cassar and his paper conservator Lousielle Bonnici confirmed, the drawings might have been done either at the time of, or shortly after, the events and the trial.

Our new friend Ken Cassar highly impressed us with his in-depth knowledge of his Museum collections and the period of the plot. Graciously, Ken gave us his permission to use our photographs of the drawings in our publications and lectures.

But what happened to Giuseppe Cohen? For his spy services, Cohen was freed from slavery, given a lifelong substantial pension, and gifted a grand mansion on Merchant Street in Valletta. Cohen chose to make Valletta his new home and converted to Catholicism to be able to run his business ventures. After Cohen's death, his descendants fought over his inheritance, and eventually, sold the mansion.

When we visited the palazzo, we found out that after Cohen's death and the sale of his estate in 1773, an organization called Monte di Pietà occupied the mansion. The Monte di Pietà is a charitable institution, which lends money to those in need at modest interest rates. Recently, the Maltese Inland Revenue Department acquired the house and rented part of the building out to a public pawnbroker.

For us, Giuseppe Cohen's story was not finished, at least not yet. We needed to see more evidence of his life in Valletta. And for that, we headed to the National Archeological Museum where we were meeting with its Chief Curator Sharon Sultana.

The Monte di Pietà building.

Right: The name of the Cohen's mansion above the entrance.

Cohen Story Concludes at the National Museum of Archeology

The Museum occupies an elegant 16th-century Baroque palazzo that used to be the Auberge de Provence. The Knights of the Order of St. John who came from Provence in France used to live there (auberge means inn). The Chief Curator, Ms. Sultana, took us through the Museum's renowned collection of Megalithic and Phoenician artifacts. I wished we could camp there at least for a week to fully explore the outstanding collections and excellently explained exhibits! I just could not pull myself away from the tiny Sleeping Lady found in the Hypogeum.

However, we had to get to the main point of our visit: the plaque from the Cohen mansion. Made from white marble in the Baroque-Rococo style, the plaque proclaimed that Di Questa Casa was given by *Gran Maestro* (Grand Master) Fr. Emanuele Pinto to Giuseppe Antonio Cohen with an important qualifier after his name: *Neofito*. *Neofito* was a designation given to a newly converted Christian. Our Giuseppe was not a Jew anymore: everyone could see that now and therefore, could fully trust Giuseppe Cohen, the Christian merchant.

The white marble plaque from Cohen's grand house.

The author (right) and Sharon Sultana, Chief Curator of the National Museum of Archeology, Malta.

The British Period (1800-1964) and the Rebirth of the Jewish Community

In 1798, Napoleon invaded Malta, banished the Order of the Knights of St. John from the islands, and freed the Jews by simply applying the laws of France: equality and abolition of slavery.

What happened to the Knights of Malta?
For the Knights, who had no intention of disappearing from history, the exile meant once again a change of location. Today, their name is the "Sovereign Military Hospitaller Order of Saint John of Jerusalem, of Cyprus, of Rhodes, and of Malta." In 1834, the Knights moved their headquarters to Rome where you can find it in the Villa del Priorato di Malta located on the Piazza dei Cavalieri di Malta.

Moreover, the Knights still have a secret or two up their sleeves. As a side note to a passionate student of history who wants to get away from the conventional touristy spots in Rome: come to that Piazza of the Knights of Malta in Rome to see the best kept secret of the Knights—the Aventine Hill Keyhole! The old green painted door on the right of the Piazza leads to the Knights' compound. The door has a very large keyhole, and you might see a few people in line who crouch down to peep through it. When you do the same, you will be amazed to see ... a perfectly framed view of the Vatican and St. Peter Basilica in the center!

What happened to the Jews in Malta?
For the Jews, Napoleon's arrival meant an opportunity to write a new page in the history of the diaspora: reconstitution of the Maltese community once again and as free people. After the dark

centuries following the forced exile and humiliation, the way was now open for the Jews to settle on the islands as free citizens.

The Rebirth of the Jewish Community

In 1800, the British drove out the French and went on administering Malta as a colony until 1964. They established English as the official language and turned Valletta into a central hub along the British trade route to Egypt, the Suez Canal, India, and the Asian Far East.

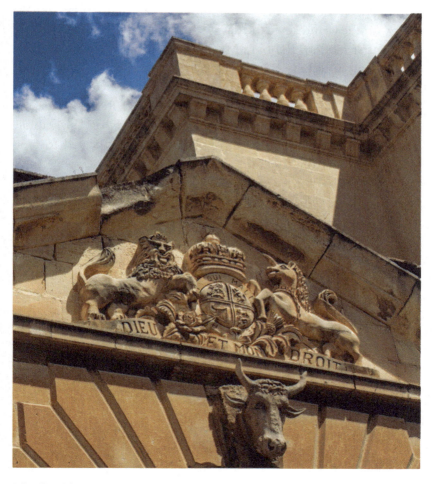

The British Royal coat of arms, like this one, is found all around Malta.

From 1798 onward, and especially under the British rule, the Jews continued arriving in growing numbers from Gibraltar, England, Italy, Morocco, Portugal, Tripoli, Tunis, and Turkey. The modern Jewish community of Malta consists mostly of the descendants of the families that came during this time period. In 1835, Sir Joseph Montefiore and his wife Judith visited Malta, met with a few Jewish families there, and generously contributed to the rebuilding of the community.

Though the community had never reached the pre-Expulsion population levels, by 1846 it had grown large enough to invite a Rabbi, Josef Tajar from Tripoli. He was the first official Jewish clergy on the island since the days before the Edict. The synagogue of the first modern Rabbi in Malta was located on the main street of Valletta, now Republic Street, but later moved to Spur Street. The 1848 revolutions in Hungary, France, and Germany brought an influx of new Jewish immigrants to Malta. Rabbi Josef and his congregation were unable to meet the needs of this rapidly growing, mostly poor, Jewish population. They appealed for and received funds from the Rabbinate of London.

Malta during World War II and the Safe Haven during the Holocaust

The only Allied base between Gibraltar, Spain and Alexandria, Egypt, Malta served once again as a military and naval stronghold. From the naval and air bases on Malta, the Allies were able to attack shipping and land targets of the Axis. This military campaign in the central Mediterranean is often called the second Siege of Malta. When the Allies opened a new front in North Africa in June of 1940, Churchill called Malta the "unsinkable aircraft carrier," knowing that defending the island was the key to preventing German and Italian control of North Africa. Hence, between 1940 and 1942, the Royal Air Force (RAF) and the Royal Navy were fighting against the air forces and navies of Italy and Germany.

As a result of its strategic importance and heavy fighting for the command of the island, Malta suffered what is considered the heaviest air bombardment in history. Across the Grand Harbor, in the three cities of Vittoriosa, Senglea, and Cospicia, the British built the Admiralty headquarters and the dockyards. Close to twenty-eight thousand people lived in an area of a half a square mile. Furthermore, Valletta was the most densely populated spot, with approximately twenty-three thousand inhabitants living within an area of a quarter of a square mile. And it is remarkable that an island, where under constant concentrated bombardment people could not venture out to find food and water for days, had become a refuge for thousands of European Jews.

The Unknown Story

During World War II, Malta was the only country that did not require entrance visas. Therefore, thanks to this "unusual"

The San Anton Palace, the official residence of the President of Malta. Photo courtesy of Joanne Grech Bianco.

immigration policy, during the Holocaust Malta rescued thousands of Jews from persecution, deportation, and death. From the late 1930s and even at the start of the war, many Jews fleeing Nazism made Malta their home, and some of them joined the British and the Maltese in the fight against the Nazis.

I was not able to find the exact estimate of the number of Jews saved by the Maltese, but only the mention of "thousands." However, I came across an article published in the *Times of Malta* in 2018 titled "Why Not Mark Holocaust Remembrance Day in Malta?" There, the author Charles Vella recalled "many" Jewish families living in his father's hotel in Sliema during World War II. In the same article, Mr. Vella lamented the absence of Holocaust education in schools that is mandatory in most other countries of the European Union. The author called the absence of both Holocaust education and commemoration of Holocaust Remembrance Day in Malta, "the virus of indifference," citing Pope Francis.

As for *Yom HaShoah* or Holocaust Remembrance Day, the President of Malta has recently instituted it. The first-ever commemoration of the International Holocaust Remembrance Day in Malta was held on January 26th, 2019 at the San Anton Palace, the official residence of the President. Peter Siegele, Director of the Anne Frank Center in Berlin was invited as a keynote speaker.

The Maltese Jewish Community Today

Ta'Xbiex Synagogue

In the late 1970s, the old synagogue in Valletta was demolished as part of a city renovation project. It took almost 20 years until, in January of 2000, a new synagogue in Malta was consecrated. It was built with the help of donors from the United Kingdom and the United States.

The new synagogue was built in the little town of Ta'Xbiex (pronounced like tash-beesh), about five kilometers (3.1 miles) from the center of Valletta. The synagogue is located on Enrico Mizzi Street on the second floor of an apartment building called "Florida Mansions."

The synagogue has a sanctuary with a central *bimah* (raised platform with a reading desk) and an *aron kodesh* (Torah ark), a room used for children's classes, and a meeting room with a long table.

Interior of Ta'Xbiex Synagogue. Photo courtesy of Mr. Ohayon.

A *mikveh* opened a few years ago. The Ta'Xbiex Synagogue also possesses a remarkable treasure: seven precious Torah scrolls. At the beginning of the 19th century, Libyan Jews from Tripoli brought one of these scrolls, inscribed on goatskin parchment, to Malta. Another scroll, housed in a magnificent silver filigree capsule, is a gift from an Iranian-English Jew.

The kosher restaurant L'Chaim established by the Chabad of Malta in 2013. Photo courtesy of Joanne Grech Bianco. Printed with permission of Chabad Malta.

One of the smallest active Jewish communities in the Mediterranean, the Maltese community has about two hundred members, and all of them live on the island of Malta.

The Chabad

The Chabad of Malta was established in the town of St. Julian in 2013 by Rabbi Chaim Shalom and his wife Chaya Segel. They also own and manage a kosher restaurant L'Chaim, very popular among Jewish visitors and native Maltese.

The Jewish Grand Master or Admor of Malta

In 2010, a controversial Rabbi named Dov Ber Hacohen moved to Malta from Israel. He proclaimed himself Admor, which is an honorific title usually given to a Jewish spiritual leader. Admor is an acronym for *Adonainu, Morainu, VeRabbeinu*, standing for "Our Master, Our Teacher, and Our Rabbi." Dov Ber Hacohen founded what he called the United Order of Light, a "non-denominational universal spiritual organization." He claims to provide blessings intended to heal emotional, physical, and psychological illnesses.

Reuben Ohayon—The Most Remarkable Personality in Contemporary Jewish Malta

Reuben Ohayon is not an ordained rabbi but he is highly regarded as a Spiritual Leader of the Maltese Jewish community in Malta, Europe, USA, and Israel. He is also a member of the European Jewish Congress, the World Jewish Congress (USA), and the Israeli Jewish Congress. A soft-spoken man with a kind and engaging smile, Reuben, who was 59 at the time of this writing, considers himself a Jew of Malta and a proud Maltese. He traces his family roots to Portugal and Morocco. His grandfather, Rabbi Nissim Ohayon, was born in Morocco and came to Malta in 1932. Reuben's father, Abraham Ohayon, was elected President of the Jewish community in 1994 after George Tajar (a descendent of the first Rabbi) passed away.

Reuben runs a successful manufacturing business in Valletta producing high-end luggage but finds time every morning to pray for at least 60 minutes in his synagogue. He is also in charge of taking care of the community's three Jewish cemeteries. Reuben was the community's official *shoichet*, but not anymore since kosher food is now imported from Belgium and Israel.

A rabbi in every sense except the official ordination papers, Reuben leads services at the synagogue. These are Sephardi

Reuben Ohayon, a true *Shaliach Tzibur*, or a Spiritual Leader of the Maltese Jewish community. Photo courtesy of Mr. Ohayon.

style services but with Ashkenazi prayer books. When Reuben talks of the synagogue, he often says: "This was my father's baby." When the old synagogue was demolished in 1979, there was no house of worship available, and people used to come and pray in the Ohayon's family apartment. Then, his father began collecting funds, and with the donors' support, bought a new place for the synagogue.

Ohayon proudly states that there is no anti-Semitism in his country of Malta. Malta's parliament now commemorates *Yom HaShoah* and on Malta's second-largest island, Gozo, a moment of silence is observed on that day.

Reuben often shows visitors the Jewish holiday themed drawings made by some of the sixty children who attend weekly classes. "They are our future," he says.

Note:

While the author and the GTA Books are solely responsible for the content of this book, the input provided by the two contributors listed below was invaluable for the parts on Malta. Joanne Grech Bianco, Historic Site Officer, Visitor Services and Events Manager for Heritage Malta, expertly guided us around Malta archipelago and facilitated our understanding of Malta today and the archipelago's complex history. Joanne's fact checking and her assistance with obtaining some much-needed photos proved instrumental for the story of Malta we wanted to tell.

Sarah Azzopardi-Ljubibratic, Ph.D. in History of Religions, a co-founder of the Tayar Foundation for Jewish Heritage in Malta, and an expert in Maltese Jewish history, provided unique insights into the medieval and the Knights' periods. Sarah had also facilitated our connections with the contemporary Jewish community of Malta and its spiritual leader, Reuben Ohayon, whose story was indispensable for the completeness of the part about Malta.

PART II
A Field Guide to Exploration of Jewish History Sites and Local Food in Malta

About this Guide and the Starting Point

This Guide is based on our in-depth research and first-hand experiences in Malta, both of which are reflected in Part I of this book. For your convenience, some of the information mentioned previously was also included in this Field Guide to assist you during the visits to the locations listed below.

You will undoubtedly discover during your trip that in Malta past is always present. As we came to believe, to walk the Jewish history path in Malta, one needs to "travel" through this country's past, one period at a time.

Choosing Your Base

We chose the Maltese capital Valletta as our starting point of our journey of discovery. Malta is small and you might decide on a different base. We made our choice because of what Valletta was: one of the most history-saturated areas in the world. Valletta, the first planned city in Europe, is only one kilometer in length (or a bit over 0.6 miles) and 600 meters in width (just under 0.4 miles), and all its straight streets lead to the sea. You will find a lot to do in Valletta. It is one of the most sophisticated micro-cities of Europe, with its many drama and opera theaters, museums and art galleries.

We suggest you dedicate your entire first day to enjoying this wondrous city: walk the streets and notice the typical enclosed balconies, visit the Grandmaster Palace, and St. John Co-Cathedral.

Map of Malta Archipelago.

After entering the cathedral, enjoy its golden interior and Caravaggio masterpieces, but you will not want to miss a marvelous bronze sculpture of Moses holding the tablets of law that stands to the right of the main altar (1567). Enjoy the Baroque splendor, but do not miss what I call the "unexpected Valletta:" Renzo Piano's striking Parliament Buildings, City Gate, and the reconstructed Royal Opera Theater.

After you have explored the Baroque Malta of the Knights and the "unexpected Valletta" of Renzo Piano, you are ready to embark on your search for Jewish stories: an exciting voyage through all layers of Maltese history.

Streets of Valletta.

The Grandmaster Palace at night.

Festival of Flowers on St. George's Square. View of the Grandmaster Palace.

Plain Baroque façade of the St. John's Co-Cathedral.

St. John's Co-Cathedral's interior.

The Parliament Buildings built by Renzo Piano. The columns of the Royal Opera House are on the left.

Finding Traces of Jewish Life during the Prehistoric Period in Malta

Recap of the Prehistoric Period in Malta

The prehistory period of Malta began with the arrival of man in the islands in approximately 5200 BCE. It concluded with the colonization of Malta by the Phoenicians around 800 BCE. The Maltese megalithic temple complexes are considered by historians to be the oldest man-made structures in the world, older than the pyramids of Giza by more than one thousand years. You fill find these strangely beautiful temples all over Malta and Gozo. However, before you board the ferry on your way to Gozo, start your "prehistoric" day on the island of Malta by visiting the Hypogeum.

Sites to Visit—Prehistoric Malta

The Hypogeum: the best place for understanding Maltese prehistory

The word "Hypogeum" means "underground." This unique structure is a maze of passages, corridors, rooms, temples, funerary halls, and a cemetery. All rooms were chiseled out of the rock sometime between 5500 and 4500 years ago.

Why visit the Hypogeum?

The Hypogeum was designed as a place of worship for the living and a burial place for the dead. Its underground architecture is well preserved over many millennia and is believed to mirror the building styles above the ground. With excellent guided tours run by the Heritage Malta experts, it is simply the very best place to gain insights into mysterious prehistoric Malta.

Only a few guided tours are allowed daily, and each group cannot exceed ten people. I bought our entrance tickets several months in advance.

Location of the Hypogeum

Address: Burial Street, Paola, PLA 1116. Telephone: 356-21-805-019. You can buy the tickets on the website: heritagemalta.org/hal-saflieni-hypogeum.

Important: We strongly suggest that in your exploration of the Jewish history in Malta you include the island of Gozo. Plan to spend a day on this amazing island. Why visit Gozo? Only there can you explore a prehistoric Ggantija temple that offers a glimpse into the world of mystery: arguably, the beginnings of the Jewish history of Malta and perhaps the entire Mediterranean. In addition, you will visit the former Jewish quarter, where the smallest Jewish community of the Mediterranean used to live in medieval times. For information on getting to Gozo and what to visit while there, see the last chapter of this guide. Meanwhile, continue your "travel" from the prehistoric period to the Phoenician period on the main island of Malta.

The Hypogeum.

Finding Traces of Jewish Life during the Phoenician Period in Malta

Recap of the Phoenician Period in Malta

This period started with the Phoenician colonization of the archipelago sometime around 800 BCE and ended in 218 BCE when Malta fell to the Romans. Phoenicians were the first recorded group to colonize Malta. They were Semitic people who lived along the coast of what is today Lebanon and Israel. They spoke a language similar to Hebrew and developed the first alphabet in the world. Great maritime traders from the Persian Gulf, they settled many Mediterranean islands and established coastal cities like Mdina in Malta. Presumably, ancient Jewish tribes like the prosperous Asher and seafaring Zebulun sailed with the Phoenicians to the Maltese islands.

Sites to Visit—the Phoenician Period in Malta

Malta National Museum of Archeology: the Phoenician Exhibit

Why visit the museum?
An excellent collection of Phoenician artifacts in the museum will deepen your understanding of these Semitic people and their contributions to our civilization. The Phoenician exhibit will also confirm that, even in the early years of the Phoenicians in the archipelago, Malta was home to a prosperous community. After all, these people were rich enough to create sumptuous sarcophagi and sophisticated decorative items.

National Museum of Archeology.

When you are visiting the museum to see its Phoenician exhibit, ask where you can find the Plaque from the Cohen's mansion. Read about Cohen in this Guide when I talk about the Period of the Knights of Malta or see the detailed discussion in Part I of this book.

Location of the Museum of Archeology
Address: Republic St., Valletta, close to the St. John Co-Cathedral.

Fishing Village of Marsaxlokk

The Maltese people are recipients of two great gifts left to them by the Phoenicians: literacy and…the "eye." The Phoenician invention, alphabetic writing, spread across the world they colonized. By the first millennium BCE, the people of the Levant, like Arameans, Hebrews, and of course the Phoenicians themselves, were using a standardized alphabet, which was later transformed into other written languages such as Greek, Etruscan, and Latin. The Maltese, just like the Hebrews, were among the very first beneficiaries of that gift of literacy. Because of the Phoenicians and the Hebrews that came with them, the Maltese language is Semitic. You hear this Phoenician gift on the streets of Malta. To see the second gift, you should travel to the village called Marsaxlokk.

Why visit Marsaxlokk village?

You might feel like you are inside some magic world when you arrive in this village. Many fishing boats anchored in the harbor are painted in the brilliant colors of red, yellow, and blue. Every boat we saw, no matter what the color, had the lower part of both sides painted reddish-brown or maroon to mark the waterline. These boats are called the *mustacc* or *moustache* because the band above the lower half of the boat is shaped like one. All boats seemed to have a life of their own, and you will feel that the boats are…well… staring at you. Yes, they all had an eye painted on their prow. This "eye" is watching over the fishermen to protect them at sea. That Phoenician legacy is alive and well in Malta after three thousand years. It is also worth mentioning that the seafood restaurants in Marsaxlokk are the best in Malta!

Location of the Marsaxlokk village

Marsaxlokk is about 7.5 miles or 20 min. drive from Valletta. The village is located in the southeast part of the island of Malta. If you do not plan to drive, take a cab or inquire about buses at your hotel.

Brightly painted boats anchored in the harbor.

Right: All boats have an eye painted on their prow. This "eye" is watching over the fishermen to protect them at sea.

Finding Traces of Jewish Life during the Roman and Early Christian Period

Recap of the Roman and Early Christian Period in Malta

The Romans conquered the Maltese islands in 218 BCE. The archipelago remained a part of the Roman Empire until the early 6th century CE. The first most renowned Jewish (by origin) visitor in Malta was the Biblical Paul who was shipwrecked on the Maltese coast in the year 60 CE. He persuaded the Roman Governor and most of the population to become Christians, so the Maltese consider him the spiritual father of the nation.

Sites to Visit—the Roman and Early Christian Period in Malta

The Catacombs of Malta

Why visit the Catacombs?
In the Catacombs of St. Paul, you will see carved menorahs and Hellenistic inscriptions: a tangible proof that a prosperous Jewish community existed in Malta in Grecian and Roman times. If you are with a guide, ask him or her to point out to you the image of a ship etched in stone: this was a symbol of the Jewish tribe Zebulun that sailed with the Phoenicians.

If you want to let the Jewish people buried in the Catacombs know that they are not forgotten, place a small stone at the exit. I did.

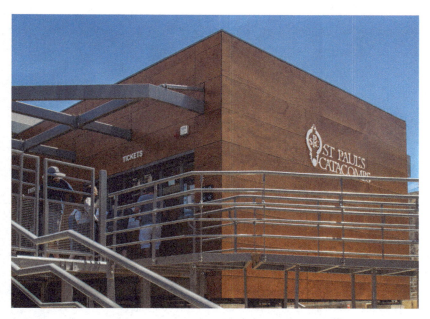

You will need a ticket to enter the St. Paul's Catacombs, Rabat, Malta.

The sign of the menorah indicates that a catacomb contains Jewish burials.

The Catacomb number is clearly marked above the entrance.

Inside the Catacombs look for the signs of the menorah.

Location of the Catacombs

Since Roman laws prohibited burials within the city limits, the Catacombs were located just outside of Mdina, Malta's ancient capital. The Catacombs are about a 20-minute drive from Valletta. You can also take public transportation: buses 51, 52, or 53. Enquire about the schedule at your hotel. Catching a cab might be easier and faster. Bring a good flashlight with you.

Address: Hal-Bajjada, Ir-Rabat, Malta.

From the Catacombs, you can catch a cab to Mdina (about a 5-minute ride to the St. Paul Cathedral in the center of Mdina) or walk via Triq San Pawl for about 14 minutes to the Cathedral located on the Archbishop Square.

Finding Traces of Jewish Life during the Medieval Period in Malta

Recap of the Medieval Period in Malta and the Dissolution of the Jewish Community

The medieval period in Malta began with the Arab occupation in 870 CE and continued until 1530 when Carlos the Fifth, the King of Spain and the Holy Roman Emperor, gifted Malta to the Knights of St. John. Under the Normans (France) and the Swabians (Germany) in the 10th and 11th centuries, the Jewish population of Malta grew to approximately five hundred families. This comprised close to one-third of the entire population of Malta's main city of Mdina.

In the 15th century, Malta became a part of the Spanish empire. So, when in 1492, the infamous Edict of Expulsion of the Jews became the law in all the lands under the Spanish crown, it also doomed the Jews of Malta. Those Jews that stayed had to convert to Catholicism, and the blossoming and rich Jewish community of Malta ceased to exist. What is left are the names: those of the streets and the conversos, such as surnames common in today's Malta like Elul (a month in the Jewish calendar) or Azzopardi (a Sephardi Jew).

Sites to Visit—The Medieval Period in Malta

Mdina—the Ancient Capital of Malta
Use the navigation app on your smart phone or ask at your hotel if they have a map of Mdina: having a map of this medieval city will be handy.

Centuries-old streets of Mdina.

A medieval palazzo in Mdina.

Above: A street sign in the former Jewish Quarter..

Above: A street in what used to be the ancient Jewish Quarter in Mdina.

Right: A street sign in the former Jewish Quarter.

The Phoenicians established the city and called it Maleth. When Arabs occupied Malta, they renamed the city Mdina, and the name stayed.

The Knights of St. John came to Malta in 1530, and they used Mdina as their central city until Valletta was built and became the capital in the 1570s.

Despite the Baroque makeover done after the earthquake that occurred in the 17th century, the walled city of Mdina masterfully preserved its medieval character. You might feel you are inside a period drama movie set. In fact, you really are! The first season of *Game of Thrones* was indeed partially filmed in Mdina.

Why go to Mdina?

Step through the gates of Mdina and walk its centuries-old streets. Remember that during the medieval period, one-third of that ancient capital's population was Jewish. Find the street with a

The St. Paul's Cathedral in Mdina.

sign "The Old Jewish Silk Market." This was a prosperous Jewish quarter, not a ghetto locked from the outside, but an open area where Jews lived, worked, and prayed.

On the central square, called Archbishop Square, you will see the St. Paul's Cathedral. The Cathedral Archives contain a collection of medieval Jewish documents, the oldest dating back to the 1300s. These documents were written in colloquial Maltese but used the Hebrew alphabet!

Location of Mdina

Mdina is about 10 km or 6 miles west from Valletta. Bus might take you there in about half-an-hour, but a cab ride, depending on traffic, will take about 12-15 minutes. To find the Jewish Quarter, look for the number 3A Carmel Street.

The Kalkara Cemetery—the Oldest Existing Jewish Cemetery in Malta

Whether you find yourself enjoying medieval Mdina or visiting the ancient Roman period catacombs in Rabat, you can hire a cab that in half-an-hour, no matter which city you are driving from, will take you to the oldest existing Jewish cemetery in Malta (established in the 1700s) located in Kalkara.

Why go to the Kalkara Cemetery?

The cemetery is closed to the public today. But if you want to walk along its overgrown paths in between ancient Jewish graves, call in advance and find out if a representative of the Jewish community might be available to let you in. Pay attention to the sign at the entrance. It is the Knights' authorization for the cemetery, a copy of which is preserved at the National Library of Malta. Translated from Latin, the sign proclaims: "This cemetery was established by the Leghorn Fund for Ransoming Hebrew Slaves, at its own expense, for the burial of the dead of the race." If you missed the story about Jewish slavery in Malta while reading Part I of this book, you will find a short version of it in the next chapter.

Entering Kalkara, the oldest existing Jewish cemetery in Malta.

The plaque on the wall of the Kalkara Cemetery. English translation reads: "This cemetery was established by the Leghorn Fund for Ransoming Hebrew Slaves, at its own expense, for the burial of the dead of the race."

The overgrown paths in between centuries-old burials at the Kalkara Cemetery.

Location of the Kalkara Cemetery

Address: Ir-Rinella, Il-Kalkara, Malta. Look for the number 4 Rinella Street, near the Church of St. Joseph.
Phone: 356-2166-5500.

Whether you are coming to Kalkara from Mdina, St. Paul's Catacombs in Rabat, or from Valletta, the taxi ride will take about the same 25-30 minutes.

Finding Traces of Jewish Life during the Order of the Knights of Malta Period

Recap of the Order of the Knights of Malta Period and Jewish Slavery

If you already visited the Kalkara Cemetery and stopped at the entrance to the oldest existing Jewish cemetery in Malta, you hopefully noticed the sign on the wall. (see the English translation on page 87). At that moment of your travel through Maltese history, you left the Middle Age behind and entered the next period, the rule of the Knights of Malta that began in 1530. That year, the Holy Roman Emperor Carlos the Fifth of Spain granted the Knights of St. John the Maltese islands as a base. The Knights based on Malta became the front line of defence against the Ottoman Turks.

To finance the fortification of Malta, the Knights waged perpetual maritime warfare, which closely resembled piracy. They captured vessels, brought them to Malta, and sold the entire crew and passengers into slavery. These prisoners were held until a ransom could be negotiated and raised. Jews were not specifically targeted, but they made up a large proportion of the merchant class. As a result, a high number of Jewish merchants were on many vessels sailing the Mediterranean. Piracy became a popular sport for the Knights, and the ransom money turned into their favorite source of income. So, there was a continuous flow of Jewish captives brought to Malta. The Knights' rule lasted until Napoleon conquered Malta in 1798 en route to Egypt. He outlawed slavery and banished the Order from the islands.

Sites to Visit - the Period of the Order of the Knights of Malta and Jewish Slavery

St. John's Co-Cathedral and the Grandmaster Palace

If you had already enjoyed the golden interior of the Co-Cathedral during your stay in Malta, you might like to dedicate a few hours now to visiting the Grandmaster Palace. There, you can visit the State Rooms and the Armory and learn more about the Order. I listed the sites directly related to the period of Jewish slavery below.

Location of the Co-Cathedral and the Grandmaster Palace

The Co-Cathedral: Triq San Gwann, Il-Belt Valletta.
The Grandmaster Palace: Il-Belt, Valletta. Very easy to reach after the visit to the Co Cathedral: 3-5 minutes' walk via St. Paul Street.

St. John's Co-Cathedral.

Grandmaster Palace.

The Jews' Sallyport

Why visit the Jews' Sallyport?

During the Knights' rule, the entire Jewish population of Malta was almost exclusively made up of Jewish slaves. Free Jews who came to Malta, often for ransom negotiations, had to seek permission from the Grand Master of the Order and could only enter and leave through a city gate called the Jew's Sallyport.

Free Jews, who came to Malta, could only enter and leave through these gates, still known today as the Jews' Sallyport.

Location of the Jews' Sallyport
Address: San Bastjan, Valletta. Look for the Fort St. Elmo bastions at the foot of the Old Bakery Street. The Jews' Sallyport is a gate in the fortifications.

Note: If you want a pleasant break from history, return to the Republic Street and turn left at Nofs-In-Nahar Street to reach the Upper Barakka Gardens. Notice the marble and bronze plaque of Albert Einstein. Then, look across the majestic Grand Harbor of Malta and enjoy the superb view of the three Maltese cities: Senglea, Vittoriosa, and Conspicua.

A marble and bronze plaque in honor of Albert Einstein. Upper Barakka Gardens.

View of the Fort of St. Angelo from the Upper Barakka Gardens.

The Site of the Slaves' Prison Building

Why visit the site of the slaves' prison building?

Slaves were kept in a slaves' prison located at the original Knights' headquarters in the town of Birgu. When a larger prison was required, the Knights built it in Valletta. Prisoners, including Jews, were allowed to work and earn money during the day. At night, they had to return to the prison. The original structure in Valletta was destroyed during World War II. What you see today while visiting this site is a memorial plaque on a modern apartment building.

The site of the slaves' prison.

Well then, why indeed go there? We, for example, specifically wanted to go there, stand near the site, and remember those Jews for whom in the 1500s Malta became a symbol of all that was cruel and hateful in the hostile world. The name Malta in Jewish literature was often associated with evil. Standing at this site, we also contemplated the enormous, highly coordinated effort to liberate the slaves organized across the Jewish world by the Jewish Society for the Redemption of Captives.

Fort of St. Angelo is on the left. The site of the slaves' prison on the right.

Location of the site of the slaves' prison building
On the map, the site is called St. Angelo Mansions, Block 4.

The Inquisitor's Palace (Museum of Ethnography) and Giuseppe Cohen

Why visit the Inquisitor's Palace?
Visiting the rooms of this palace is a unique experience that will provide insight into the inner mechanisms of the Inquisition. The Inquisition Office in Malta was established in 1561 and abolished by Napoleon in 1798. During these centuries, only around one hundred cases were recorded involving Jewish defendants from among

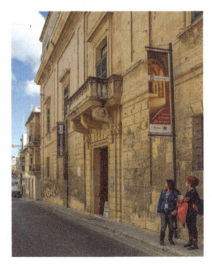

The entrance to the Inquisitor's Palace and the National Museum of Ethnography.

Above: The Inquisition Tribunal inside the Inquisitor's Palace.

Right: Inside the Torture Chamber

the slave prisoners. Those Jews were charged not with Judaizing, which was the worst crime for the Inquisition, but with such offenses as blasphemy. This was the Roman Inquisition, which, unlike the Spanish one, seldom sentenced prisoners to death. During its existence in Malta, no more than seven death sentences total were documented.

When buying your entrance tickets, ask if the recently donated collection of the 18th-century "slaves' plot" drawings is already on display. If the drawings are indeed available for viewing, you will have a great opportunity to learn about the most remarkable Jewish personality in Malta during the period of slavery: Giuseppe or Joseph Cohen. He is credited with saving Malta from the Turks in 1749.

Read about Cohen in Part I, Chapter "Guiseppe Cohen, the Most Remarkable Personality in Malta During the Period of Slavery." The Museum's 19 drawings done during the time of the plot depict in great detail the capture of the conspirators, interrogation, trial, and execution.

Location of the Inquisitor's Palace
Address: Triq Il-Palazz Ta' L-Isqof, Birgu BRG 1023, Malta. The town of Birgu (also called Vittoriosa) is about 5.5 miles from Valletta.

Giuseppe Cohen's Mansion: Monte di Pietà

For his courageous actions, Cohen was freed from slavery, granted a lifelong substantial pension, and given a grand mansion on Merchant Street in Valletta. Cohen chose to make Valletta his new home and converted to Catholicism to be able to run his business ventures. After Cohen's death, his descendants fought over his inheritance, and the mansion was sold. After the sale of his estate in 1773, the organization called Monte di Pietà, a charitable institution, moved in.

When you are visiting the Museum of Archeology and enjoying its Phoenician exhibit, ask if it is possible to see the Plaque from the Cohen's mansion. If you are able to view the marble plaque, note the word *Neofito* that follows Cohen's name. A newly converted Christian was called *neofito* or *converso*.

The Monte di Pietà building gifted to Giuseppe Cohen for his spy services.

Right: The name of Giuseppe Cohen's mansion is still visible above the entrance.

Location of Giuseppe Cohen's mansion
Address: 46 Merchant Street, Valletta.

Finding Traces of Jewish Life during the British Period in Malta (1800-1964)

Recap of the British Period in Malta (1800-1964)

Napoleon invaded Malta in 1798. He banished the Order of the Knights of Malta from the islands and abolished slavery. The Jews of Malta were finally free.

Then, in 1800, the British took Malta from the French, and it remained a British colony until 1964. After the arrival of the British, the Jews continued coming in growing numbers from Gibraltar, England, Italy, Morocco, Portugal, Tripoli, Tunis, and Turkey.

For the most part, the modern Jewish community of Malta dates back to those times. The first Rabbi of Malta, Joseph Tajar of Tripoli, arrived in 1846. The first synagogue was located on the main street of Valletta, now Republic Street. Later, it moved to a building on Spur Street. When that building was demolished, the synagogue moved first to Ursula Street, and later to the town of Ta' Xbiex. You will find information about the Ta' Xbiex synagogue a few pages later.

British Royal coat of arms.

Finding Traces of Jewish Life in Malta during World War II

Recap of Maltese History during World War II and the Safe Haven during the Holocaust

During World War II, Malta became once again a military and naval stronghold, serving as a base for British military operations against the Axis naval and land targets in the central Mediterranean. In 1940-1942, the RAF (United Kingdom's Royal Air Force) and the Royal Navy were fighting against the air forces and navies of Italy and Germany.

Malta experieced heavy air bombardment. Valletta was the most densely populated spot with its 23,000 people living within an area of a quarter of a square mile.

In spite of the extremely dangerous situation, the fact that Malta became a refuge for thousands of European Jews is nothing short of a miracle.

This was possible because during World War II, Malta was the only country that did not require entrance visas. Consequently, during the Holocaust, Malta rescued thousands of European Jews. We do not know how many lives were saved by the Maltese. What we do know is that the Maltese people, who, while suffering under bombardments and deprivations, opened their hearts and their doors to thousands of persecuted Jews.

You will not find a monument dedicated to the Holocaust in Malta. But the courageous and generous deeds of the Maltese people speak for themselves.

Sites to Visit—Malta during World War II

The war history enthusiast might spend an entire day in these three museums:

The Malta at War Museum
The museum is set in the former army barracks and in a cut-out-of-the rock air shelter. This museum is dedicated entirely to Malta's role during World War II.

Location of the Malta at War Museum
Birgu (Vittoriosa), Malta.

The Lascaris War Rooms
These rooms are the former War Headquarters from which the Allies conducted their operations. These rooms are situated in an underground complex of tunnels.

Location of the Lascaris War Rooms
Valletta, Malta. When you are in the Upper Barakka Gardens, you can reach the Lascaris War Rooms within a one-minute walk.

The National War Museum
This museum explores the entire military history of Malta focusing on the most famous victory of the Knights over the Turks, the Great Siege of Malta in 1565.

Location of the National War Museum
Fort St. Elmo, Valletta, Malta.

The Maltese Jewish Community Today

Sites to Visit—Maltese Jewish Community Today

The Island of Malta

Ta'Xbiex Synagogue

The Ta'Xbiex synagogue is located in the little town of Ta'Xbiex (pronounced like tash-beesh), about five kilometers (3.1 miles) from the center of Valletta. The synagogue has a sanctuary with a central *bimah* and an *aron kodesh*, a room used for children's classes, and a meeting room with a long table.

If you visit the synagogue, make sure to see the Torah scrolls. One of them is inscribed on an ancient goatskin parchment. This Torah was brought to Malta from Tripoli by Libyan Jews at the beginning of the 19th century.

Interior of the Ta'Xbiex synagogue. Photo courtesy of Reuben Ohayon.

Contact Mr. Reuben Ohayon at his work office far in advance of your visit and ask for an appointment and to see the synagogue: Ohayon Travelling Goods Center & Co LTD at 356-2123-7309 or send him a message via Facebook: facebook.com/Ohayon-Travelling-Goods-Center-LTD-MALTA.

Location of the Synagogue of Malta
Address: Enrico Mizzi Street, Second floor of an apartment building called "Florida Mansions," Ta'Xbiex, Malta.

The Chabad of Malta
In 2013, Rabbi Chaim Shalom and his wife Chaya Segel established the Chabad of Malta in the town of St. Julian on the island of Malta. They also own and manage a kosher restaurant L'Chaim, a very popular eating establishment among Jewish visitors and native Maltese.

Location of the Chabad of Malta and the Restaurant
Address: 83 George Borg Olivier St., St Julian's, Malta. Reservations required for the restaurant. Call: 356-7774-1888.

A popular kosher restaurant L'Chaim established by the Chabad of Malta in 2013. Photo courtesy of Joanne Grech Bianco. Printed with permission of Chabat Malta.

The Islands of Gozo and Comino

To continue your exploration of Malta (the country), you will need to take a ferry from the port of Cirkewwa located on the island of Malta and sail across the Gozo Channel to the island of Gozo. It is a short trip that will take about forty-five minutes. About half-way across the channel, you will see a small island of Comino on the starboard (right) side of the ferry.

A Gozo Channel Line ferry at the Cirkewwa port.

Passing the Island of Comino on the Way to Gozo

Ask a local to point out the island of Comino to you. This tiny island of just 1.4 square miles with a population of total three people is located about halfway between the islands of Malta and Gozo. In spite of its tiny size, Comino has an illustrious place in Jewish history be-

A Gozo Channel Line ferry.

cause of one Jewish sage who lived there from 1285 until 1291. His name was Avraham Abulafia (1240-1291). A visionary philosopher

 far ahead of his time, Abulafia founded the school of "Prophetic Kabbalah" and dreamed of resolving the differences between Judaism, Christianity, and Islam. Read about Abulafia in Part I of this book.

Islands of Malta, Comino, and Gozo.

View of the island of Comino from the ferry.

View of the island of Gozo from the ferry.

Ggantija Temple—Entering the World of Mystery on the Island of Gozo

Make sure you leave yourself enough time to enjoy this island. Gozo is very small, even by Maltese standards: its seven thousand people live within 26 square miles. After disembarking from the ferry, you enter the city dominated by the massive Citadel built by the Knights of St. John. You should not miss the citadel; however, your main focus is of course Ggantija or the temple built by the Giants, as the local population used to call it for centuries.

Entrance to the Ggantija Temple.

Why visit Ggantija?

Ggantija is a perfect example that illustrates the intricacies of prehistoric architecture. In addition, Ggantija will offer you a glimpse into the world of mystery: arguably, the beginnings of the Jewish history of Malta and perhaps the entire Mediterranean. You might need to ask Heritage Malta staff at the entrance for directions to find what was previously considered to be stone-hard evidence of the ancient Jewish presence. It is located not far

The prehistoric Ggantija Temple in Gozo.

from the inner apse of Ggantija: the inscription in two lines and ten words, seven words in the first line and three in the second. When translated into English from what was Hebrew written in the Phoenician alphabet, this inscription reads: "To the love of our Father Jahwe" or in some sources, the translation reads: "My father YHWH." The "YHWH" stands for Jahwe or the God of Israel.

Did the first Jews of Malta arrive in Gozo over three thousand years ago and scratch their prayers in stone using the Phoenician alphabet? Be prepared for the staff to disappoint you: since 2013, the current opinion of the Heritage Malta is that this inscription is a 19th-century forgery. Forgery or not, it is possible that Jews did arrive in Malta with the Phoenicians.

Location of the Ggantija

From Valletta, you might need a cab to get to the Cirkewwa port to board a ferry for a forty-minute crossing across the Gozo Channel to the island of Gozo. From there, if time is an issue, we suggest taking another cab. Otherwise, you can take a public bus. Check the ferry and bus schedules at your hotel before you go.

The inscription on the wall of the Ggantija's Temple is hard to see. The photo shows it as seen when standing in front of it.

Address: Triq John Otto Bayer, Ix-Xagħra, Gozo, Malta. But you do not really need it: as soon as you say "Ggantija" everyone will know where you want to go.

Jews in Medieval Gozo

While exploring the ancient capital city of Gozo, find what is believed to be the pre-Expulsion Jewish Quarter.

Ask a local to direct you to the Cathedral of the Assumption located in the island's capital, Victoria. The street named Triq IL-Fosos (the Ditch Street) along the north side of the Cathedral will lead you into the area of narrow medieval streets and ancient buildings. Look for a plaque on the wall indicating the location of the Jewish Quarter in medieval times.

The tiny Gozo community consisted of only eight large extended families. However, the community played an important, disproportionate to its size, role in the island's economy. The Jews of Gozo paid taxes to the City University and held a monopoly as apothecaries and dyers. Today, neither the exact location of the synagogue or that of the local Jewish cemetery is known. Stand for a few minutes in the middle of the Triq IL-Fosos street and imagine

The Cathedral of the Assumption in Victoria, Gozo. The old Jewish Quarter was located along the north side of the Cathedral.

a bustling Jewish neighborhood that along with its inhabitants was destroyed after the Edict of Expulsion.

Left: The street sign Triq IL-Fosos, meaning Ditch Street, indicates the area where the Jewish Quarter in Gozo is believed to have been located.

The Jewish Quarter in Gozo's capital Victoria.

Exploring Culinary Treasures of Malta

Disclaimer: All addresses and contact information are accurate as of the time of writing.

Eating Kosher in Malta

Restaurant L'Chaim
When the Chabad of Malta was established in the town of St. Julian in 2013, the Rabbi Chaim Shalom and his wife Chaya Segel decided to open a kosher restaurant. They now own and manage L'Chaim, an Israeli-style eatery, whose name embodies an expression of bringing people together and wishing of blessings and peace. The L'Chaim is very popular not only among Jewish visitors but also with native Maltese. The restaurant is located on Georg Borg Oliver Street in the town of St. Julian. The phone number is 356-7774-1888.

However, when you are in Malta and you do not follow kosher laws, you should not overlook another treasure of this magic island: the amazing local food specialties, many of which reflect Maltese history.

Not Always Kosher—but Oh So Tasty...

Oh Food! Glorious Maltese Food!
Alex and I do not observe kashrut. For those who are also not very strict with their dietary choices, at least when they travel, we compiled a list called "Do not leave Malta without trying..." There, we placed Maltese bread and pies right at the top! In this "category," we considered the *hobz*, *ftira*, and *pastizzi* to be the prizewinners.

So many choices!

Hobz, a traditional local bread, reminded us of sourdough bread, our favorite back home. And, as we learned, it was also prepared in a similar fashion by using leftovers of yesterday's dough to leaven today's loaf. We loved to eat it in a manner that the locals call *hobz biz-zit*, when you rub the crust with olive oil and fresh tomatoes. Some like to pile up tuna, capers, and onions on top, but we loved it just like that: pink in color and delicious!

Pasta with great local seafood.

Aljotta – traditional tomato-based seafood soup with lots of garlic.

And then, there is *fitra*, disc shaped and semi-flat, resembling our traditional pita bread. *Fitra* is a living reminder of the ancient Jewish history in Malta: it is kosher and the recipe dates back to medieval times, when the Jews constituted about thirty percent of the island's population. While having lunch in Café Cordina, we tried fitra stuffed with olives, capers, and anchovies, all mixed in a piquant tomato sauce, or rather a paste, made locally from sun-dried tomatoes, rosemary, and sugar. Incredible!

But what we cannot forget are small pies called *pastizzi* made of flaky pastry. The recipe goes back to the Arab occupation of Malta (ninth to eleventh century), and now exists in two main varieties: cheese and parsley or peas and onion—both equally mouth-watering. We saw *pastizzi* sold everywhere in Malta in what are called *pastizzerijas* or take-out-only tiny shops. We tried to find these *pastizzi* in the US and have them shipped to us, but in vain, until my Google search fetched me Malta Joe's Baked Goods in Tucson, Arizona, which ships their goods nationwide. Have yet to call in and order.

The soups, we noticed, are very popular all over Malta. *Minestra* is a close cousin to minestrone from nearby Italy, but two other soups, uniquely Maltese, stand out. The "Widow soup" or *Soppa tal-armla*

Local restaurants invite you to select the fish you want to have prepared.

Aljotta, here I come!

received its name from cheap and simple ingredients that for some forgotten reason should be green or white, like cauliflower or spinach. We saw it served with a poached egg and a piece of ricotta cheese. The second soup that I especially liked was the *Aljotta*, which is a tomato-based fish soup with lots of garlic.

The main course in Malta, like in the US, often includes either seafood or meat dishes. And of course, on this Mediterranean island, seafood is simply glorious! Grouper, sea bass, or what I especially liked—the octopus—were my favorites.

We are not big on meat dishes, but one dish deserves a special mentioning: the *fenek* or rabbit. During the rule of the Knights of St. John, who loved rabbit hunting, the locals were prohibited from catching those annoying rabbits that ate farmers' crops. But thanks to Napoleon, who sent the Knights packing, the Maltese turned *fenek* into a local favorite dish. I doubt the rabbits appreciated the change. The Maltese beloved holiday is the Feast of St. Peter and St. Paul. And the celebrations are not complete without a *fenkata* or a rabbit dinner consisting of various rabbit dishes. When our daughter was little, her favorite books were Beatrix Potter's Peter Rabbit tales. So, no, we did not try any rabbit dishes in Malta!

Saving the best for last: desserts! I personally could not let a day go by in Malta without having at least a few of their wonderful pastries. Desserts in Malta, like most of the local specialties, reflect the island's historic influences. The cannoli, which most probably came from Sicily, called *kannoli* by the Maltese, are sold everywhere. My favorites were the *kannoli* filled with candied fruits. Arabic in origin, Maltese *qubbait* or nougats were excellent, especially when made with almonds or hazelnuts.

Tantalizing pastries seem to greet you at every corner.

The *gaghh tal-ghasel,* honey or molasses dough rings, are unique to Malta. They are traditional treats for Christmas, we were told, but available all year around. We liked them best with our morning coffee. But for me, the crown princess of the Maltese desserts was the *mqaret,* an elegant almond-shaped cookie with spiced dates and—oh so sinfully—deep fried. Our friend Joanne told me that these were the best with vanilla ice cream. Forget the ice cream, I thought, finishing up my bag of *mqarets.*

Select Movies Filmed in Malta

Malta has many surprises, and one of them is that since the late 1970s, this tiny archipelago located in the center of the Mediterranean has transformed itself into a center of the movie production industry. And we are not talking only about the European and US filming companies. India, the subcontinent renowned for its beautiful historic monuments and exotic scenery, has recently begun choosing Malta as a shooting location for its blockbuster movies. The latest Indian movie, shot right before the Pandemic in March 2019, was *Bharat* starring popular Indian actors Salman Khan and Katrina Kaif.

Cinematographers often transform Maltese islands into ancient Troy, Greece, or Rome. Watch, for example, *The Odyssey* directed by Andrei Konchalovsky in 1997 with Isabella Rossellini and Christopher Lee; Ridley Scott's *Gladiator* shot in 2000 with Russell Crowe, and Wolfgang Petersen's 2004 *Troy* with Brad Pitt as Achilles, to name just a few. All these movies were filmed in Malta's Fort Ricasoli located at the south entrance to the Great Harbor. Built by the Knights of St. John in the 17th century, this fort, three hundred plus years later, served as an imposing central square of Troy, the massive Colosseum of Rome, or even as a threatening Turkish prison for the 1978 Alan Parker's *Midnight Express*. Steven Spielberg's *Munich* (2005), a movie telling the story of Mossad agents hunting terrorists all over Europe, was almost exclusively shot in Rabat and Valletta on Malta.

The question is—why Malta? Of course, Malta is astonishingly, breathtakingly beautiful. However, this is not the only reason for scores of moviemakers to choose the archipelago to represent various places around the world for big and small screen productions. The answer is contained in the three letters—the

MFS, or the Malta Film Commission, a government body set up in 2000 with the goal of encouraging the production of films in Malta and promoting the archipelago as a filming location. The clever encouragement and promotion include multiple financial incentives, tax credits, and production co-cost coverage (of those films that meet Malta's cultural test criteria).

In addition, the Malta Tourism Authority also offers financial and logistical support to film and television productions that choose to film locally depicting "Malta as Malta." As stated on the MFS website, this successful strategy led to more than 200 million Euros in foreign direct investment into Malta's economy over the last six years prior to the Pandemic.

Below we listed a few films we liked where, in addition to enjoying the film by itself, you might also recognize some iconic Maltese landmarks.

First, the color of the Mediterranean Sea around Malta is neon-blue or azure. You will recognize it immediately in the movie *Kon-Tiki* (2012) directed by Joachim Ronning and Espen Sandberg. This Oscar-nominated film was about legendary Thor Heyerdahl crossing the Pacific on a small raft to prove his theory that Polynesia was settled by South Americans. Well, instead of the Pacific, you will be looking at the sea surrounding Maldives and Malta!

The iconic Maltese landmarks, such as the Grand Harbor and the village Marsaxlokk, appear in the film *Capitan Phillips* directed by Paul Greengrass in 2013 and nominated for six Oscars. The islands of Gozo and Comino "perform" in the 2015 romantic film *By the Sea* directed by Angelina Jolie, and starring Brad Pitt and herself. The main characters (Jolie and Pitt) go diving in Comino and sail on a private yacht to Victoria, the capital city of Gozo.

The Grandmaster Palace is easily recognizable in the 2016 film *13 Hours: The Secret Soldiers of Benghazi* (director Michael Bay). You will also see it in the early movies like *The Count of Monte Cristo* (2002, with Jim Caviezel, Guy Pearce, and Richard Harris, directed by Kevin Reynolds), and the British film *Revelation* (2001, directed by Stuart Urban with James D'Arcy and Natasha Wightman).

St. John's Co-Cathedral, Marsaxlokk, Great Harbor, Malta International Airport, Fort St. Elmo, and many other landmarks appear in multiple movies, but one of the most memorable sites is probably the ancient capital of Malta, the medieval Mdina that became a location for the widely popular *Game of Thrones* (2011-2019). One landmark, however, that was featured in numerous movies, including *Game of Thrones*, does not exist anymore. That was the Azure Window in Gozo, a twenty-eight-meter-tall (ninety-two feet) natural limestone arch rising from the sea. The imposing rock formation, beloved by visitors and Maltese alike, collapsed during a storm in March 2017. But you can still "visit" the Azure Window while watching some movies I mentioned above: *The Odyssey*, *The Count of Monte Cristo*, and *Game of Thrones*, to name a few.

PART III
Corsica: The Island of Beauty, the Island of the Just

Why Should Jewish History Buffs Go to Corsica

Corsican Surprises

The Jewish story of Corsica is not well known, and many are surprised to hear that the island has any to reveal. However, in 1763, Corsica was the first modern country to proclaim social and political equality for the Jews during the island's short-lived republic (1755-1769): twenty-seven years ahead of the United States and twenty-eight years ahead of France. In addition, the island's Jewish narrative uncovers a secret power of Omerta (the Mafia's code of silence) that led many Corsicans to risk their lives to save thousands of Jews who fled Nazi-occupied France during the Holocaust.

Corsica wears many "hats": nicknamed *Kalliste* ("the most beautiful") by the ancient Greeks, it is called "the Island of Beauty" by modern day vacationers and "the Island of the Just" by the French Jews. Snuggled between two crown jewels of the resort world, the French Riviera and the Italian western shore, Corsica, however, is not on the travel map of many globe-trotters. Yet that island's untamed natural magnificence is arguably the Mediterranean's best.

Corsica is also a treasure trove of fascinating historical information. The island's strategic position right in the middle of the western Mediterranean attracted waves of invaders: the Carthaginians, Greeks, Romans, Vandals, Goths, and Saracen Arabs, to name a few. Corsica is an enigmatic world with many

Corsica is located between two crown jewels of the resort world, the French Riviera and the Italian western shore.

and varied appearances: from the prehistoric menhirs (man-made standing stones) and intimidating Genoese citadels to the light-reflecting granite rocks and dense dark forests. "This wild island is more unknown and more distant to us than America, even though you can see it from the coasts of France," wrote famous French writer Guy de Maupassant in the 1830s. Not much has changed in this respect. However, for those who venture to explore it, Corsica unveils its fascinating secrets, one mystery at a time.

The Last Untamed Corner of Europe
"Imagine a world still in the midst of chaos, a tempest of mountains separating narrow gorges in which torrents flow..."
Guy de Maupassant

The revered 19th-century writer was fascinated by Corsica, and a number of his novellas were inspired by this island, such as "The Corsican Bandit" and "Happiness" among others. As a dedicated fan of his books, I am sure Maupassant would not stand for some of his countrymen's ages-long exasperation with the incorrigible Corsicans. This negative attitude, my French cousins told us, is best expressed in the well-known French wisecrack: "We should cut the mooring ropes and push it (Corsica) out into the sea." Well, it is true, as my husband Alex and I discovered crisscrossing the island, that many Corsicans do not like the French much and think they should not belong to France. So, the feeling is mutual. We, however, fell forever in love with the island and its history, people, and their spirit.

I came to believe in Corsica's generous heart. If you seek it, you will certainly find the island's true essence: when walking the streets of the picturesque hilltop villages and charming medieval towns, while visiting elegant Pisan churches and threatening Genoese fortifications, or along the Corsican rugged coastlines and breathtaking viewpoints—there lies the Corsican heart. And for history buffs striving to uncover the island's Jewish narrative, it is crucial to understand what made Corsicans … well … Corsicans.

Map of Corsica.

Corsica in Prehistoric Period

With that goal in mind, we needed to travel back in time, deep into Corsican prehistory, 8000 BCE, which in our modern world is translated into a thirty-one mile drive south of Ajaccio or fifty-two miles northwest of Bonifacio. We were looking for Filitosa, the most famous prehistoric site in Corsica, administered with loving care by our new friends: Charles-Antoine Cesari, the director of the site and a member of the family that owns it, and Maria Shelepova, the events manager. It was Charles-Antoine Cesari Senior, the grandfather of our friend, who, while working his land in 1946, made the first discoveries of what proved to be a treasure trove of architectural and sculptural artifacts, a window into a mysterious prehistoric Corsican civilization and the people who created it.

The author (center) with Charles-Antoine Cesari (right), the Director of Filitosa and a member of the family that owns it, and Maria Shelepova (left), the events manager.

Statue-menhirs. Photo courtesy of Charles-Antoine Cesari.

The Mysterious Menhirs and Sardinian Relations

Charles-Antoine and Maria met us at the entrance to the Cesari's family-owned estate, the home of the National Historical Monument Site, Filitosa, one of the largest among the European megalithic prehistoric areas. Filitosa's claim to fame is its puzzling statue-menhirs that Grandfather Cesari had discovered. Menhir is a man-made upright standing stone, like in Stonehenge for example. Only in southwestern Corsica, most of them are anthropomorphic: each one has a chiseled face, and they are all armed with a sword-like weapon. To distinguish the anthropomorphic menhirs from the much older, man-made upright stones, those that we see in Filitosa are called statues: statues-menhirs. In Filitosa, they all have different facial expressions. And so it was that under their gaze and, as we hoped, caring protection, our journey into the Corsican story had begun.

Walking through Filitosa was an almost surreal experience: there were only a few visitors in that vast area, and we felt like we were inside a world before Time. Everywhere, in the meadows and in tree groves, in between the ruins of strange round stone houses and towers, we seemed to be followed by the statue-menhirs. Their

All menhirs in Filitosa have different faces, and their human features transform them into armed warrior heroes.

human features (faces, shoulders, and arms) carved into their granite façades transformed them into armed warrior heroes or gods.

The archeological investigations in Filitosa began in the 1950s, when Charles-Antoine's grandfather invited a renowned French scholar, archeologist Roger Grosjean. The museum in the park has excellent exhibits illustrating the site's long history of continuous settlement from the ninth millennium BCE until the third century BCE, when Corsica came under Roman control. The dizzying variety of archaeological finds is accompanied by detailed English-language explanations. Charles-Antoine has recently written to me that in August 2020, they opened a much larger brand-new museum.

Even today, the scientists do not agree on the affirmative answers. Who were the creators of those enigmatic statues? What was their purpose: ceremonial, healing, or commemorating historical events? And how are these mysterious sculptors-builders related to modern day Corsicans?

The ruins of what looks like the *nuraghe*, a round-in-shape tower-fortress type of construction, very similar to the prehistoric building remains in Sardinia.

The Corsican prehistory is considered to begin with the Pre-Neolithic period, sometime around 9000 BCE, when, as historians suggest, hunters from Sardinia crossed the Strait of Bonifacio to settle in Corsica. In 566 BCE, the Greeks colonized Corsica and called it Kyrnos. We don't know the name of the island prior to the Greeks' arrival. With the Greeks, Corsica transitioned from the Bronze Age to the Iron Age and to history proper, or recorded history. We learned that Corsica and nearby Sardinia (both Greek colonies at that time) formed one province within Magna Crecia. Likewise, the Romans, who came next, considered these two islands, closely tied both geographically and culturally, *Provincia Sardinia et Corsica* or Province of Sardinia and Corsica.

Historians believe that modern Corsicans are named after an ancient people known by the Romans as *Corsi*, who gave their name to the island. These people most probably originated from the northeastern part of Nuragic Sardinia. Perhaps, it was the Corsi who brought the Nuragic culture from Sardinia to Corsica. The adjective nuragic is derived from Sardinia's most characteristic monument, the *nuraghe*, a round-in-shape tower-fortress type of construction. The ancient Sardinians built those structures all over their island starting from about 1800 BCE until the Roman conquest in 238 BCE. Ruins of similar structures could be found in southwestern Corsica and in Filitosa. In Corsica, those similar to the Sardinian buildings are often called the *torri* or towers, and that Bronze Age megalithic Corsican civilization was named the Torrean.

It was in Filitosa that Corsican prehistory taught us an important lesson, the one all Corsicans have imprinted in their hearts and minds even before they are born. Not only that their island is made of the same landmass as Sardinia but also, as their civilization, history, culture, and mindset are concerned, Corsicans have much more in common with Sardinia than, say, with France or Italy.

A genetic study published in 2003 stated: "Corsica...appears to be greatly differentiated from the populations of regions such as France and Tuscany .... The Mediterranean population most comparable to Corsica is Sardinia." (Vona, G.; et al. "Genetic Structure and Affinities of the Corsican Population: Classical Genetic Markers Analysis." *American Journal of Human Biology*, 15 #2, pp. 151–163, 2003). In addition to the common genetic makeup of their people, both Corsica and Sardinia have a similar culture of proud and fierce independence. Independence movements, against the Italian federal government in Sardinia and against the French authorities in Corsica, are the central forces within the islands' politics.

The Sherden Warriors—Ancestors of the Corsican Independent Spirit

The second lesson that Corsican prehistory taught us was that the Corsicans' ancestry connected them to the ancient rebellious tribes of the Sherden (or Shardan) warriors, also called the Sea People. Roger Grosjean dedicated over twenty years of his career researching Corsica's megalithic period. He wrote that the Torrean civilization in Corsica began when, at the end of the second millennium BCE, the Sea People known as the Sherden, landed on the island, possibly, from the western Mediterranean like Sardinia. The Sherden subdued and eventually melted into the native megalithic population. Grosjean thought that it was the Sherden who built the *torri* and erected the armed statue-menhirs to represent their heroes.

The Sherden are thought to have been sea raiders, pirates, fearless warriors, and mercenaries offering their services and fighting skills to local employers, including Mycenaean (Greek) lords and Egyptian pharaohs. As we learned, most scientists today see the Torrean civilization we encountered in Filitosa as the result of a local evolution that began in the Neolithic period with Sardinian cultural influences.

I am tempted to see a direct line from the proud and independently minded Corsicans we met in May of 2019 to their Sherden ancestors. After all, I have the backing of a powerful historical personality. Yes, it was none other than the Egyptian Pharaoh Ramesses II, who reigned from 1279 until 1213 BCE! One Rameses' rhetorical stele states: "As for the Sherden of rebellious mind, whom none could ever fight against, who came bold-hearted, they sailed in, in warships from the midst of the Sea, those whom none could withstand..." (Kitchen, Kenneth A. *Ramesside Inscriptions Translated and Annotated: Ramesses II, Royal Inscriptions*. Cambridge: Wiley. p. 120, 1996.)

Our next step in exploring the Corsican story was Corte, widely considered the cradle of Corsican independence.

The Cradle of Corsican Independence

"We are Corsicans by birth and sentiment... As Corsicans, we wish to be neither slaves nor rebels... Either we shall be free or we shall be nothing..." Pascal Paoli, Letters. Quoted in Thrasher, *P. Pasquale Paoli: An Enlightened Hero, 1725-1807*. London, Constable, 1970.

Going to Corte
The town of Corte is literally the heart of the island, both culturally and geographically. If you have time for visiting just one inland town in Corsica, I strongly suggest it should be Corte. No other place in Corsica offers such an in-depth understanding of this island and the mindset of its people. Corte lies on the N193 road and is about thirty-four miles from Ajaccio.

Our drive took us across the Col de Vizzanova, a mountain pass in the inland valleys, and splendid views accompanied us all the way to Corte. In the southwest and northwest parts of Corte, we admired how the town seemed to be guarded by tall craggy mountains. In the northeast, we enjoyed the views of the beautiful hilly area with a multitude of tiny picturesque villages descending towards the coast. Driving to Corte allows for a perfect time to reminisce about the succession of great powers fighting one another throughout history in their quest to control the island.

The Succession of Powers
The Romans ruled Corsica for almost seven hundred years, until the Vandals occupied it in 430 CE, followed by the Byzantine Empire a century later. Charlemagne, the Holy Roman Emperor, conquered Corsica in 774 CE. From that time on, the fight for control of the island against the Saracen Arabs lasted for about three hundred years. In the 11th century, Corsica was transferred

to the Papacy, and the Italian city-states took over. In 1077, Pope Gregory VII granted the island to Pisa. In 1133, Pope Innocent II divided Corsica between Pisa and its archrival, Genoa, with Genoa acquiring full control of the island in 1284.

All over Corsica, you see the Romanesque-style churches built by the Pisans, while the Genoese, who favored Baroque for their churches, were mostly focused on defensive structures, like citadels and watchtowers. The Genoese ruled for five hundred years, with some interruptions caused by the takeovers, first by Spain (1296-1434) and then by France (1533-1559).

The Corsicans often revolted against the foreign powers. In the 18th century, the island was in a state of almost continuous warfare against the Genoese, until in 1755, the people of Corsica led by Pascal Paoli announced their independence and created the Corsican Republic.

You can feel the proud spirit of nationalism all over the island, but especially when driving to Corte. It is impossible not to notice directional signs with French town names blackened out and handwritten instead in the Corsican language.

The Moor's Head is the symbol of the island's independence.

The symbol of the island's independence, *La Tête de Maure* (the Moor's Head) follows you around everywhere: from cars' license plates to souvenir shops and graffiti on buildings. In Corte, this image—a young black man's profile with a white bandana in his hair—is truly ubiquitous and as integral to the city as the legacy of its heroes.

The City as a Symbol of Corsica

Corte was originally a fortress, ruled alternatively by the Aragonese, Genoese, and French. However, in 1755, when the Republic of Corsica was proclaimed, Corte became the birthplace of Corsican patriotism. The Republic lived for only fourteen years, but its influence over the spirit and mindset of the Corsicans cannot be overestimated: Corte has forever become the symbol of the island and its struggle for independence. For Jewish history enthusiasts, Corte is also the place where the Corsican Jewish story had begun. The establishment of the Republic and that of the safe haven for the Jews in Corsica were in many respects possible due to the leadership, political genius, and enlightened mind of one man, Pascal Paoli (1725-1807).

The Father of the Nation

We walked along Cours Paoli, the main street in Corte named after the most revered hero in Corte's history. It was early May, still the school term time, and Corsican-speaking students crowded bars and restaurant terraces. Just a day prior, we flew in from France where we had spent a week. Though administratively Corsica is considered a part of France, here was a strikingly different world. The strong sense of Corsican cultural distinctiveness pervaded the streets.

We stopped by the *Fountaine des Quatre-Canons* (Fountain of the Four Cannons). This medieval-looking structure was actually built at the end of the eighteenth century, in 1778, when the Corsican Republic had been dead for nine years and Corsica was French. Louis XVI commissioned the fountain to channel water from the mountain torrents to the local garrison, which was stationed in Corte to deal with those incorrigible Corsicans.

At the foot of the upper town, we approached Place Paoli, a large square surrounded by lovely nineteenth-century buildings, mostly cafes and restaurants. We entered one of them to have a delicious espresso and took our seat right in front of the large monument to Pascal Paoli, the island's beloved hero. To refresh what we had learned about him in preparation for this trip, we opened up a book I had in my backpack: *The Journal of a Tour to Corsica and Memoirs of Pascal Paoli* written by the eighteenth-century Scottish scholar and one of the earliest Grand Tour travelers James Boswell and reprinted by Turtle Point Press in 2002. The author knew Paoli personally, and I thought this was the best contemporary account of the Corsican leader's life available in English.

A passionate advocate for Corsican independence, a committed patriot, and a talented military strategist, Pascal Paoli became

The Fountain of the Four Cannons.

known as *Il Babbu di a Patria* or the Father of the Nation. He distinguished himself in leading Corsicans in their fight against Genoa and France, established an independent democratic state, wrote its Constitution, and founded the University of Corte, just to mention a few of his nation-building accomplishments.

Paoli was a son of a physician and patriot Giacinto Paoli, who became one of the three "Generals of the People" in the Corsican

Monument to Pascal Paoli.

nationalist movement. Pascal was five years old when his father fought against the Genoese; he was fourteen when his father took him into political exile in Italy. His older brother, Clemente, remained at home as a liaison between the exiles and the Corsican People Assembly. At the age of 29, Pascal Paoli had already won trust and respect among the Corsican exiles and rebels at home, when he devised a sound plan for a native Corsican independent government.

In 1753, a hero of the Corsican independence struggle, Jean-Pierre Gaffori of Corte (1704-1753), a medical doctor by training, a general, and one of the "Protectors of the Nation" triumvirate, was assassinated in an ambush on the streets of his town. Hence, there was an urgent need for a capable leader in Corsica. In 1754, through a popular election Paoli was chosen to become the General-in-Chief of Corsica and take charge of all resistance groups. He stepped right in to lead his island toward becoming an independent country.

Paoli, who received an excellent classical education while in Italy, was a cultured and enlightened man. He proclaimed Corsica a sovereign nation, founded the Corsican Republic in 1755 as a representative constitutional democracy, created an administration and justice systems, founded an army, outlawed bloody vendettas, created a free public school system, and established a university—all based on the principles of Enlightenment.

As a President, Paoli held his office by election and not by appointment, which made him a chief public officer as well as a commander-in-chief. Though he led his people to overall victory over the Genoese, the Italians still held a few coastal cities and their citadels; but the Corsican Republic controlled the rest of the island from the inland mountain town of Corte, its capital city.

The Constitution, the Flag, and the University

Paoli wrote the first Corsican Constitution inspired by the Enlightenment philosophy of Jean-Jacques Rousseau, who was later commissioned by Paoli to write the *Projet de constitution pour la Corse*, (Constitutional Project for Corsica) in 1763. One of the most democratic constitutions at the time, the Constitution of Corsica included the first ever implementation of female suffrage. The document was written in Tuscan Italian, the language of cultural elite in Corsica then. Ratified the same year, 1755, the Constitution was in existence until the French invaded Corsica in 1769 and forced Paoli into exile in Great Britain.

Paoli was also instrumental in adopting the Moor's Head as a national emblem and a flag of the Corsican Republic. In a curious wink of history, that emblem was brought to Corsica in the thirteenth century by invaders, the Aragonese kings, who wanted newly conquered people, the Corsicans, to see them as victorious over the Moors in Spain. It is interesting to mention that the bandana originally covered the Moor's eyes and was raised to the forehead by the independent Corsicans to symbolize the island's liberation.

The University of Corsica is named after its founder. Just like the Constitution, the University did not survive the short-lived Republic: it was closed after only four years in 1769 by the French. Under pressure from the Corsicans, the University was "re-founded" and opened again in 1981, more than two hundred years after it was first established. The only university in Corsica, it has secondary campuses in Ajaccio, Biguglia, and Cargèse.

Walking the Independence Trail in Corte

We left Place Paoli to follow the route I had planned back home and called the "Corsican Independence Trail." Heading west from Paoli Square, we came to the ramps Rue Scolisca that led us to the heart of Corte and Place Gaffori. We circled the large statue at the center: the monument to another renowned hero of Corsican independence I mentioned earlier, Jean-Pierre Gaffori.

Corte's native son, Gaffori became one of the "Protectors of the Nation" triumvirate, the

Ramps Rue Scolisca leading to the heart of Corte: Place Gaffori.

bravest leaders of a major insurrection against the Genoese in 1745-1755. Gaffori managed to take large territory of the island from the Genoese before he was killed in an ambush in 1753. His wife Faustina fought courageously next to her husband. According to the local legend, when one of their sons was taken hostage and used as a human shield by the enemy, she urged the hesitating patriots into attack by exclaiming: "Don't think about my son, think about your country!" She was immortalized on one of the base reliefs on the pedestal of the monument to her husband.

The house where the Gaffori family lived stands behind his statute, opposite one of the town's oldest buildings, the 15th-century Eglise de l'Annonciation church. The Gaffori house

Monument to Jean-Pierre Gaffori, another Corsican hero. Gaffori's house, pitted by countless Genoese musket bullets, is behind the statue.

façade is pitted by the Genoese musket bullets fired during their desperate fight to hold Corte in 1746.

Leaving the Place Gaffori, we headed towards the Citadel built by the Genoese in 1419. This citadel had become a symbol of the islanders' fight for independence, especially when Pascal Paoli established the first Corsican University there. The Citadel houses the Musee de la Corse, the best historical museum on the island and a must for any history aficionado. The historical archives, the art institute, and a tourist office are also located inside the Citadel.

Going toward the upper town and the Citadel.

Right: The doorway to the Palais National on Place du Poilu.

We first stopped a few hundred feet from the entrance to the bastions of the Citadel, on the Place du Poilu to visit the Palais National. This seventeenth-century building served as a residence of the Genoese governors of Corsica.

When the Republic was proclaimed, the mansion became the residence of the young nation's President, Pascal Paoli. This was where independence was declared and the sovereign state was born. For the next fourteen years, Palais National was the seat of the new Corsican parliament. Now, fittingly enough, the building houses the Institute of Corsican Studies, which is a separate branch of the University of Corsica,

Bastion at the highest point inside the Citadel.

while other departments and specialty schools are located inside the Citadel.

The End of the Republic

In 1768, the Genoese, though having officially renounced all claims to Corsica, sold the island to France. Duc de Choiseul, the minister of the French Navy, bought it on behalf of the Crown. The Treaty of Versailles that confirmed the Genoese sale of Corsica to France was signed on May 15th 1768. The treaty stated that "Corsica may never become sovereign and independent or possess any… maritime establishment that could prejudice the navigation." In September of that year, France began its conquest of Corsica.

May 8th of 1769 is considered by Corsicans *La Fin d'un Reve* or the "End of a Dream." On that day near the bridge at Ponte-Novo, the republican army led by Pascal Paoli was defeated by the overwhelming French forces. The Ponte-Novo battle ended the fourteen years of independence, the only time in their history when the Corsicans were not dominated by other nations.

Paoli had to leave for England. He returned in 1794, when the British intervened on Corsica's behalf and created a short-lived Anglo-Corsican Kingdom. But in 1796, the French troops led by a young Corsican, Napoleon Bonaparte, retook the island. Paoli once again left for England, and Corsica has remained French ever since. Paoli died in 1807 and was buried in Old St. Pancras Churchyard in London. In 1889, his remains were brought back to his beloved island and interred at the family estate in Stretta, Morosaglia commune, Haute-Corse. A Cenotaph and a marble bust of the Corsican hero were placed in Westminster Abbey in London.

The American Connection

Very few Americans visit Corsica, and even those who do typically know very little about its history. So, it was a big surprise for me to find out that the name of the greatest Corsican hero, Pascal Paoli, could be found on the map of the United States, and more than once. Not just one, but six states have a town named after him. There are towns called Paoli in Colorado, Indiana, Kentucky, Oklahoma, Pennsylvania, and Wisconsin.

If you drive west from Philadelphia for 45 minutes via I-76 W, you come to the town of Paoli, PA, where—if you are a history buff—you may find out about the Paoli Massacre, a battle in the Philadelphia campaign of the American Revolutionary War fought on September 20, 1777. That battle is sometimes called the Battle of the Paoli Tavern. The town itself was named after "General Paoli's Tavern," a meeting spot of the Sons of Liberty, who named that tavern as a homage to the great man they called the "General of the Corsicans."

Corsica and the Jews

When a persistent and passionate historic travel aficionado comes to Jewish Corsica, drives around the island, walks the streets, meets and talks to people, he/she will begin to feel with the heart and mind what the Corsican universe and those who created it are all about. The history of the Jews in Corsica goes back at least a millennium.

The Early Jewish Communities

Historians believe that around the year 800 CE, a large group of Jewish families arrived from Egypt in what is Porto-Vecchio today. Most settled in an inland mountain village aptly named Levie by the locals. Were the Jews hiding from their persecutors and attempting to get away from the coast? We might never know. What we do know is that the newcomers spoke and wrote in Hebrew; there are documents written in Hebrew in some ancient village churches in that mountainous region.

The Levie village exists today, and is located inland, 43 kilometers (26 miles) from Porto-Vecchio and 57 kilometers (35.6 miles) from Bonifacio. If you are staying in Bonifacio, then driving on D59 from there to Levie will take no more than an hour, the same time as from Porto-Vecchio on D368.

Staying in Bonifacio is one of the most memorable aesthetic experiences of a lifetime. During all our days of driving along the Corsican "carousel" that we developed trying not to miss any of the main sites, we were falling deeper and deeper in love with the raw beauty of this island. But we left our hearts in Bonifacio. This city extends over the tops of limestone cliffs and its superb magnificence comes from the imposing medieval fortress and upper town houses that look toward Sardinia on one side and over

Bonifacio the Magnificent.

its harbor on the other. Indeed, this stunning city oversees the most beautiful harbor in Corsica, supposedly admired by Homer and described in his *Odyssey*: "We put into that port, so well-known amongst sailors: where sheer double cliffs, with no gaps, encircle the harbor and two headlands squeeze the narrow entrance in their grasp." (*Odyssey*, Chapter X). Was Homer the first Bonifacio tourist? Whether he was or not, Bonifacio is simply awe-inspiring.

While staying in Bonifacio, a Jewish history aficionado would be conveniently located for an enjoyable day trip visiting both Porto-Vecchio and Levie. In Porto-Vecchio, you will find a beautiful yacht-filled marina and the most gorgeous beaches. In the mountain village still called Levie, you will enjoy its ageless romantic charm. However, no Jews live there today and have not for centuries. Those Egyptian Jewish immigrants intermarried, assimilated, and disappeared into Corsica. I call their arrival and eventual melting into Corsica "Phase 1" of the Corsican Jewish story.

"Phase 2" began in the early 1500s, when over one thousand Jews arrived from the south of Italy. Most were from Naples, and all were fleeing the persecution after the infamous Edict of Expulsion

Bonifacio upper town. Houses at the edge of the limestone cliffs.

of 1492. Running away from the Inquisition, these refugees settled in the mountainous regions in the center of the island. It is not known if the descendants of the sixteenth-century *Italiani del Sud* (Southern Italian) refugees were still in Corsica and lived as Jews by the end of the 1600s. In 1684, after violent pogroms in the Padua ghetto, many Jews from that renowned center of Jewish learning had to escape from Italy. At that time, Padua was a part of the Republic of Venice; Venetian attitude towards the Jews is well presented by Shakespeare in his *Merchant of Venice*.

However, Corsica had always been a world apart from the rest of Europe. The *Italiani del Nord* (Northern Italian) newcomers were welcomed and nicknamed Padovani to indicate their origin. That "Phase 2" of the Corsican Jewish story ended the same way as "Phase 1." Jewish immigrants from both the south and, later, the north of Italy and their descendants intermarried with the local population and assimilated. But the surname Padovani is very common in Corsica even today.

The Jews of Paoli

"The Jews have the same rights as Corsicans, since they share the same fate."
Pascal Paoli.

The "Father of the Nation" to Corsicans, Pascal Paoli had also become "the Father" to the Jewish community of the Republic he created. He was an enlightened leader, who firmly believed in human rights and political and social equality for all.

I came across an 1889 volume of *The Menorah: A Monthly Magazine for the Jewish Home*, where a historian Charles A. Bratter in his extensive essay *Pascal Paoli: Patriot and Hebrophile* analyzed a series of Paoli's official decrees, preserved in the collection of the Bibliotheque du Louvre. Bratter stated that Paoli "sets forth the most enlightened and humane ideas on the question of equality of the religions, and shows himself absolutely free from the narrow prejudices of his age" (Volume VII, July-December 1889).

During the fourteen years of the Republic, Paoli brought to Corsica several thousand Jews from northern parts of Italy and Spain, mostly from the west coast of Tuscany and from Catalonia. I call these events "Phase 3" that represents the beginning of the modern Corsican Jewish narrative.

The estimate of the exact number of people who came with the late 18th-century wave of Jewish immigration varies greatly, depending on the sources. For example, the article on the Corsican Jewish history published in *Tribune Juive* on August 26, 2015, cited the total number of these newcomers in the range between five and ten thousand during all the years of the Republic's existence.

Another authority, a French historian Antoine-Marie Graziani in his book *Pascal Paoli: Pere de la Patrie Corse* (Father of the Corsican Homeland) stated that in one year, 1767, six hundred

Jews, or probably about one hundred and twenty families, arrived in L'Île Rousse (Tallandier, Paris, 2002).

There were some Jews in L'Île Rousse even before the arrival of those 120 families. Among the Paoli letters in the Corsican archives, there is a mention dated 1763 of a Jew in L'Île Rousse, an immigrant from Livorno, named Modigliani. That man requested to benefit from the same right to vote as other Corsicans. The President of the new republic was whole-heartedly in favor of that request and proposed to create a Jewish colony in Corsica with the same rights as other Corsican citizens enjoyed. It is tempting to fantasize that the bold requester of political rights might be an ancestor of another rebel from Livorno with the same surname, a genius artist of the 20th century, a painter called Amedeo Modigliani (1884-1920).

L'Île Rousse, a commune in the northwestern part of Corsica, was founded by Paoli in 1758 in order for the Republic to have a port that was not ruled by the Genoese, who, at that time, still controlled some ports on the island. For example, the nearby big port Calvi was still loyal to the Genoese.

L'Île Rousse is only 24 kilometers (about 15 miles) from Calvi, which is now one of the most popular vacation destinations on the island due to its beautiful marina and overall natural magnificence.

From Calvi to L'Île Rousse is less than a 30-minute drive. The town, located by a beautiful bay with its white sand beaches and reddish-colored stone islets, has recently become a Riviera-style resort. Most tourist brochures mention that the red islets around L'Île Rousse are the reason for the town's name.

However, I came across some sources, such as a quotation in *Tribune Juive*, that the town received its name from … the Jews! Most of these immigrants' names were hard to pronounce for the locals, and they nicknamed the new arrivals, some of who had red hair, "*Rossu*," which means a "redhead" or plural "*Rossi*." We were told that the surname Rossi is widespread among the Corsicans.

There is no affirmative answer to the origin of Paoli's port name. What we do know for sure is Paoli's purpose. He clearly understood that the young nation, after being exploited by the

Calvi marina. Arguably, Calvi boasts the most beautiful marina in Corsica.

Calvi Upper Town.

Genoese for five hundred years, needed to build a firm economic foundation. This is where Jewish merchants were indispensable. Graziani quoted Paoli's letter from 1760 to Domenico Rivarola, the consul of Piedmont (north Italy) asking him to contact "accredited rabbis" in the area and assure them that "if the Jews wanted to settle among us, we would grant them naturalization and the privileges to govern themselves with their own laws."

Many of the Jewish entrepreneurs, who decided to come to Corsica seeking new business opportunities along with religious freedom, were from Livorno. At that time, Livorno was a European Sephardic city second in importance only to Amsterdam, both in the size of its prosperous Jewish population and in business growth. It was well known throughout Europe that the Jews of Livorno held a monopoly on the coral trade and a significant share of the diamond trade as well.

In 1767, to create an attractive business incentive, Paoli authorized the Jews of Livorno to fish for corals along the Corsican coast. In the 1769 book by Paoli's Scottish friend James Boswell, there is a mention of the exchange of Corsican coral for British weapons that were sent to Paoli's army (J. Boswell, *The Journal of a Tour to Corsica and Memoirs of Pascal Paoli*). Paoli indeed counted on the immigrant Jews to help develop the Corsican economy and on the British to support the new republic militarily.

The Corsicans, we learned, have always been opposed to public displays of religion, and they never differentiated between those who were native to the island and the strangers, even with a different religion. A young man, who was a manager at our hotel in Ajaccio, told us that the word "Jew" did not exist in the Corsican language.

The Corsicans' natural inclusiveness might be the explanation for many mixed marriages and almost total assimilation of the Jews there throughout the centuries of Jewish immigration. What I call "Phase 3" of the Corsican Jewish story had ended the same way as "Phases" 1 and 2. The Jews, who melted into Corsica, left behind the widespread surnames like Giacobbi, Padovani, Rossi, Simeoni, and the geographic names of tiny inland villages, like

Levie and Casalabriva (*Casa di Ebreo* or "the House of Hebrew"). Even though in the last thirty or so years, historians began to argue over the origins of these surnames—Hebrew versus Christian—there is also a popular opinion that almost 30 percent of Corsicans might have some Jewish blood.

Ajaccio, Napoleon, and the Jews

"We all are heirs to Judaism."
Napoleon Bonaparte

Having traveled for years throughout the Mediterranean, we thought we became used to its splendor. However, Ajaccio, surrounded by wild mountains and azure-colored sea, was simply spectacular. We were not alone in being so impressed by Ajaccio's location: famous French writers, like Guy de Maupassant and Prosper Merimee, were also captivated by the city's setting.

Ajaccio is divided into three very different sectors: the oldest (a Genoese-built town with its medieval streets and the Citadel), the

Ajaccio, surrounded by the wild mountains and azure-colored sea, is one of the most picturesque locations in the Mediterranean.

modern sector with its broad boulevards, and the suburbs with great views of the sea. The city has an unmistakable imperial look and should be a must destination for any history enthusiast. After all, this is where Napoleon Bonaparte was born (1769) and raised.

We visited Ajaccio in May of 2019, but I wish we were there again in August of that same year, when the city had a grandiose celebration of the 250th birthday of its most illustrious son. I also wish it would have been possible for us to fly to the island of Saint Helena in 2021, where Napoleon died in exile. There, on May 5th, multiple commemorative events and conferences were planned in honor of the 200-year anniversary of Napoleon's death in exile. Due to the COVID 19 pandemic, these plans were moved to spring 2022.

In Jewish history, Napoleon is one of the greatest heroes. He was the government leader whose Civil Code of 1804 granted religious freedom to all people, including the Jews. Napoleon spearheaded the emancipation of the Jews of Western Europe bringing the ghetto walls down during the Napoleonic Wars (1804-1815). It was on Saint Helena, that on November 10th 1816, Napoleon explained to his doctor Barry O'Meara why he consistently supported political and social freedom for the Jews: "I wanted to free the Jews to make them full citizens ... I insisted that they be treated as brothers since we all are heirs to Judaism." (Ben Weider, Ph.D., a Napoleonic scholar and founder of the International Napoleonic Society. "Corsica and the Jews," *AgoraVOX*, August 23, 2010).

In Ajaccio, one meets Napoleon everywhere. We walked along the Cours Napoleon, the main boulevard that crosses the entire city and is frequently intersected by small alleys leading down to the sea or up to the hills. We came to the Maison Bonaparte, the house where Ajaccio's hero was born, now a museum that displays a couch on which Napoleon's mother gave birth to him.

We stopped at the Place de Gaulle that is dominated by the monument to Napoleon on horseback dressed like a roman emperor and surrounded by his four brothers in Roman senatorial togas.

Above: The memorial plaque commemorating the birthplace of Napoleon.

Left: The bust of Napoleon in his family mansion.

Monument to Napoleon on Place de Gaulle.

I am a life-long collector of historical curiosities. And since Alex and I are naturalized United States citizens, originally from Russia, I remembered a few rather remarkable coincidences that connected a country where we were born, the country we chose to be our homeland, and ... Napoleon's brothers. His brother, Joseph, as a Minister of Plenipotentiary, negotiated a peace treaty with the United States in 1800. The youngest brother, Jerome, was involved in Napoleon's disastrous Russian campaign of 1812: as the King of Westphalia, he mobilized an army and commanded a corps marching towards Minsk (now in Belorussia).

But it was Jerome's grandson who provided the strongest U.S. connection: Charles Joseph Bonaparte served as the United States Secretary of the Navy and the United States Attorney General in President Theodore Roosevelt's administration, 1901-1909. In 1908, Charles Joseph established a Bureau of Investigation that grew under J. Edgar Hoover into the modern-day F.B.I.

After reminiscing about Napoleon's siblings, our search for places connected with his life continued. We were looking for the street running parallel to the sea, Cours Gandval, which leads to the Place d'Austerlitz. An imposing monument called U Casone dominates the square and commemorates Napoleon's victories. His statue is on the top of a small hill: the emperor wears his renowned two-cornered hat. This is a copy of the famous statue placed in front of Napoleon's memorial in Les Invalides in Paris.

There is one more place in Ajaccio that I consider of high importance for all history aficionados, whether they are interested in Napoleon or are in search of a Jewish story.

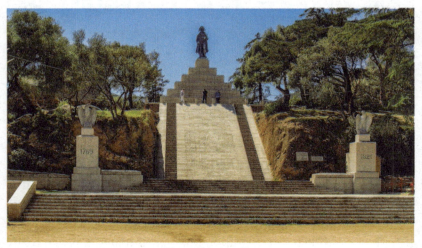

Place d'Austerlitz.

Napoleon statue at Place d'Austerlitz.

My husband and I are passionate art lovers, who visit any art museum we ever come across in our travels. However, the one in Ajaccio was on our not-to-miss list for a number of different reasons. This museum is not only the best in Corsica but it also contains the second most important collection of Italian paintings in France after the Louvre.

Musee des Beaux-Arts of Ajaccio is located in the Palais Fesch, the palace built by Napoleon's uncle Cardinal Joseph Fesch (1763-1839). He was a highly knowledgeable collector and dedicated three of the building's wings to display his art collection. By the time Joseph Fesch became a Cardinal and moved to Rome in 1803, he owned over 16,000 works of art.

For dedicated museum-goers, I mention just a few examples of the pieces Cardinal Fesch collected. Later, many of these works of art became star treasures in some of the best museums around the world: in the National Gallery of London—*The Entombment* by Michelangelo, *Mond Crucifixion* by Raphael, and *Adoration of the Magi* by Bramantino; in Gemaldegalerie, Berlin—*Last Judgement* by Fra Angelico. In the U.S.A., we have *Hunting in the Lagoon* by Vittore Carpaccio at the Getty Museum, and *Saints George and Domenic*, side panels from an altarpiece by Carlo Crivelli at the Metropolitan Museum of Art. In July of 2019, the Metropolitan had an exciting exhibit focusing on another Fesch piece, Leonardo's unfinished masterpiece *Saint Jerome in the Wilderness* that came from the Vatican Museums.

For Jewish history seekers, here is an interesting detail about Joseph Fesch, Napoleon's uncle. The uncle was only six years older than his ambitious nephew, and for some time, Fesch was close to Napoleon and supportive of his brilliant political and military career. However, their relationship soured greatly for a number of reasons, with one of them being ... the Jews! As quoted by a renowned Napoleonic scholar Dr. Ben Weider, the Cardinal told Napoleon: "Do you know the Holy Scriptures predict the end of the world when the Jews are recognized as belonging to a Christian Nation as equals?" The Cardinal refused to participate in the coronation ceremony when Napoleon became the emperor, saying: "Sire, you wish the end of the world to come with you giving the Jews equality..." (Ben Weider, "Corsica and the Jews," *AgoraVOX*, August 23, 2010).

I thought it was only fitting for the twentieth century Corsican Jewish story to begin in the city that gave the world one of the most passionate champions of the Jews. I call it "Phase 4" of the Jewish narrative in Corsica.

Cardinal Joseph Fesch's statue occupies the center of his palace's courtyard.

Jews in Corsica in the 20th Century

The first two decades of the twentieth century ushered in what I call "Phase 4" of the Corsican Jewish story. One of the reasons we came to Ajaccio, the island's largest city and its capital, was to explore the place where the 20th-century narrative of the Corsican Jewry had its beginnings.

Ajaccio—"A Stopover in the Storm"

While researching the Corsican Jewish history, I came across an extensive essay by Florence Berceot describing the influx of Jewish refugees arriving in the Corsican port Ajaccio from the Middle East in 1915-1920 (*Cairn Info Jewish Archives,* 2005/1, Volume 38). So, after visiting the Palais Fesch, we headed to the Ajaccio port.

Today, most cruise ships dock at the Gare Maritime on Quai L'Herminier, which is around 300 meters (almost 1,000 feet) north of the main tourist office on Place Foch, Ajaccio's main square. Arriving at the port, I thought, was an entrance to a new safe life for the twentieth century Jewish refugees. Berceot called her piece "A Stopover in the Storm," and provided an excellent overview of the turbulent events in the Middle East during World War I that displaced uncounted thousands of people and brought a few thousand "Israelites" to Ajaccio. Those were the Jewish families from the French mandated countries, like Syria and Lebanon, escaping the agonizing world: the once powerful Ottoman Empire was descending into chaos and falling apart.

The Syrian and Lebanese Jews disembarked from a French military boat in Ajaccio in December of 1915. They followed the 700 or so Algerian and Moroccan Jews, who, in summer of the same year, chose to leave their once comfortable lives behind and immigrate rather than, as the Turks requested, renounce their French protected status. The French allowed those Jewish refugees

Ajaccio port.

to come to France, but not quite: all were sent to Corsica, the island of poverty and "misery," as the author of the "Stopover" described. Many of them came to Ajaccio.

As it happened in the previous centuries, Corsicans, despite their own deprivations, eagerly opened their cities, hearts, and wallets to the destitute refugees who were prohibited by the Ottomans to take with them any savings or possessions. In his "Les Juifs en Corse" (The Jews in Corsica) article, Claude Benasouli described how the prefect of Corsica Mr. Henry assisted the mayor of Ajaccio Mr. Pugliesi-Conti in organizing accommodations for the newcomers. An unoccupied Catholic seminary was quickly remodeled to provide each family with a separate dormitory room, an auditorium was transformed into a synagogue, a *mikveh* or a ritual bath, was installed, and even (somewhat) kosher food was provided (*Tribune Juive*, #1179, Nov. 15-20, 1991). The teachers in school, where the Jewish children were enrolled, had accepted a pay cut of their already modest salaries in order to collect the money for their students' clothes.

At that time, a small Jewish community had already been living in Bastia since the early twentieth century. Most of the families in Bastia had emigrated from Tiberius. So, sometime after arriving in Ajaccio, some Jews, mostly Moroccan families, left for Bastia. Many other families followed later.

Seeking Stability in Bastia

Bastia, the second largest city in Corsica after Ajaccio, is the island's military headquarters and its economic capital. During the fourteenth century, the Genoese turned an ancient fishing village into an important fortified town when they built their fortress there. The name of the city comes from *bastiglia* in Italian that translates into English as "fortress." Located on the northeastern coast, 22 miles south of Cape Corse, Bastia's port is one of the busiest French ports in the Mediterranean. Just 73 miles from Livorno, the city is very close to Italy. In good weather, the locals say, one can see the island of Elba across the Tyrrhenian Sea, the place of Napoleon's first exile in 1814.

The old town of Bastia or Terra Vecchia, with its medieval-looking alleys and vaulted passages is located around the harbor. The Terra Nuova or the upper ("new") town is looming over the harbor with its threatening citadel and the elegant Palais des Gouverneurs that was the home of the Genoese governors for centuries. Now, the Palais houses a fine museum of Bastia history, Musee de Bastia.

The arrival of new members of the Jewish community to Bastia during World War I prompted substantial organizational changes: the Israelite Cultural Association of Bastia was formed in 1916, and a larger space for the synagogue had to be found. If Jewish sojourn in Ajaccio was very short, the community in Bastia proved stable. By 1918, the Jewish refugee population exceeded 800 people. When World War I was over, some families returned to their homeland; but by the end of the 1920s, and especially, in the early 1930s, most of them came back to Bastia, along with many newcomers—all fleeing the deadly violence and the economic crisis in their home countries.

In 1934, the Synagogue Beth Meir was founded in an apartment, located in number 3 Rue de Castagno, in the historic part of the city. Today, with the exception of Chabad centers, Beth Meir is the only synagogue in Corsica. Its name, Beth Knesset Beth Meir, was chosen as a tribute to Rabbi Meir, a philosopher mentioned in the Mishnah. Rabbi Meir Toledano (1889-1970) was the community's rabbi from 1920 until his death in 1970.

The diminishing community consists of a few elderly families, and the services are held only on Shabbat and during the holidays. An article "The Last Kaddish of the Jews of Corsica" by Antoine Albertini published in the *Le Monde* magazine on September 1, 2007, lamented that the 20th-century small but strong community is all but disappearing in the first decade of the 21st century. The blessing of the wine was done with beer, because no kosher wine was available. The last grocery store, which was authorized to sell kosher products, closed due to the lack of customers. The once-a-week Hebrew classes taught by a retired real estate agent were attended by a Franciscan monk and nine elderly ladies that patronized charities at the Saint Anthony Convent.

Why didn't these few remaining Jews of Corsica leave the island? The author of "The Last Kaddish" quoted the answer he received from the daughter of Rabbi Toledano, then in her eighties: "What location in the world where Jews have been more welcome than in Corsica?"

Interior of Beth Meir Synagogue, Bastia. Photo used with the permission of the ANU Museum of the Jewish People, the Oster Visual Documentation Center. Courtesy of Louis Davidson, Synagogues 360.

Jews in Corsica during World War II

"We must always take sides. Neutrality helps the oppressor, never the victim."
Elie Wiesel

For most of World War II, Corsica was occupied by 80,000 Italian soldiers, later joined by 15,000 Germans. People in Bastia did their best to hide their Jewish neighbors, many of whom were living there since the early 20th century. However, under the German pressure, part of the Jewish community in Bastia was rounded up and interned at a camp in Asco, a small commune in the Haute-Corse. Thanks to the continuous protection of Paul Balley, the island's powerful wartime prefect, none of them were deported to Nazi concentration camps in continental Europe. After the liberation, all were released.

The "Righteous Island"

On June 17, 2010, *The Jewish Chronicle* (a London-based Jewish weekly newspaper) published an article by Marcus Dysch, "Corsica Shock over the Discovery of its only Holocaust Victim." The newspaper described how a Corsican teacher Louis Luciani uncovered a tragic story of one Jewish man who actually was deported from Corsica. His name was Ignace Schreter. Schreter first fled from Germany to France and then from France to Corsica, but was reported to the French authorities in the autumn of 1942. Schreter was deported to Sobibor and eventually murdered.

As Luciani discovered, that event took place during a short absence from the island of its strongly pro-Jewish prefect Paul Balley. One of Balley's low level staffers took an opportunity to report on the only Jew he knew about. An elderly official told Luciani that he remembered how furious the prefect was when he found out what had happened to the Jewish refugee. Legendary Nazi-hunter Serge Klarsfeld stated that Paul Balley deserved the "Righteous among the Nations" title, since he protected the Jews in Corsica while risking his own life.

About ten years ago, an official request was made by the Corsican authorities that Yad Vashem, the World Holocaust Remembrance Center in Israel, recognize Corsica as a "Righteous Island," similar to the designation earlier requested by the Denmark Resistance members.

To find out the status of that request from Corsica, I contacted Yad Vashem and received a detailed response from Dr. Joel Zisenwine, the Director of the Righteous among the Nations Department. Dr. Zisenwine stated that, first of all, "contrary to the common notion, Denmark did not receive collective recognition" of a Righteous among the Nations country. Instead, individual people of Denmark and Denmark Resistance fighters were honored by the trees planted in Yad Vashem.

Concerning Corsica, Dr. Zisenwine noted that, over the years, his Department received various inquiries regarding the rescues of Jews on that island during the Holocaust. However, no precise circumstances of rescue efforts, testimonies, or firsthand account of survivors were provided. As Dr. Zisenwine explained, Yad Vashem mandates that the "Righteous among the Nations" honor could be only given to individuals who risked their lives saving Jews, not the country or the island (email from January 3rd, 2021).

I wish that could be changed: while Denmark was the only country in Europe that saved almost the entire Danish Jewish community, Corsica was the only region of France that wholeheartedly protected the Jews seeking refuge there.

Corsica as a Safe Haven during the Holocaust

During World War II, France under Marshal Petain undertook a widespread census of the population, which was used by the Nazis to round up the Jews and send them to the death camps. Some of those who were lucky to escape fled to Corsica. Vichy government documents discovered after the war showed that almost no Jews had been reported in Corsica and turned over to the Nazi authorities.

Corsican officials continuously and consistently reported that they had no Jews on the island and therefore had no one to report on. However, thousands of Jews were sheltered in Corsica. As quoted in the groundbreaking report printed by *Le Figaro* in 2010 about the heroism of Corsicans, one prefect wrote to a Vichy official: "I have the honor of being able to inform you that none of my military sector leaders were able to find any Jews that were being hunted under the government's criteria." (Quoted by Michael Cosgrove in "The Secret Story of the Jews Saved by Corsica in WWII," *Digital Journal*, October 27, 2010).

The Secret Power of Omerta

Omerta is the code of silence and honor by which all members of illegal organizations like Unione Corse (Corsican mafia) abide. *Omerta* categorically prohibits cooperating with authorities, such as representatives of the government or law enforcement, and requires maintaining complete silence when being questioned by them.

It was the combined power of the mafia's honor code and the ever-present, organically Corsican compassion for fugitives from persecution and injustice that inspired so many Corsicans during World War II to risk their own lives to save the lives of others. An untold number of thousands of French Jews (mostly from southwest France) found a welcoming refuge in Corsica, where they were saved from certain deportation and death on the mainland.

Corsicans used multiple tricks to keep the concealed Jews away from some zealous officials or locals. For example, some village mayors issued false identity papers and ration cards; if any of the refugees raised suspicion, that person was quickly transferred to a different village with a new identity paper. In some mountain villages, the hidden Jews were declared to be of Turkish or of some other neutral country origin.

There were hundreds of similar stories that remained unknown to the new Corsican generation. As stated in Cosgrove's article, an association was founded to honor those many villagers that hid the Jews during World War II. The JDD Journal (*Le Journal du Dimanche*), a Sunday magazine in France, published a piece about the 2010 documentary made by Andre and Clementine Campana. In that film, the documentarists took the viewers from one village to another to discover and celebrate the families that hid the Jews during the Nazi occupation. There, one man stated about his grandmother: "She was not hiding a Hebrew. She was hiding a persecuted person." This is how Corsicans are made, concluded the film.

Back to the Question: What Made Corsicans—Corsicans?

"Between Corsica and the Jews, it's a story of the soul."
Didier Meir Long, author of the *Memoires Juives de Corse*, Lemieux, 2016.

I found a fascinating article about Didier Meir Long in *L'Arche*, a French Jewish news magazine. There, Naoemie Halioua, a renowned journalist, interviewed Mr. Long, a former Benedictine monk from Corsica, who converted to Judaism. He became a historian focused on early Christianity, Jewish spirituality, ancient wisdom schools, and ... Corsican Jewish history. Halioua herself became famous when she published her book *L'Affaire Sarah Halimi* about the 2017 vicious murder of a French Jewish woman that French authorities resisted calling a hate crime. So, thanks to Google translator, I was able to follow the captivating conversation between the two bright Jewish minds.

Mr. Long explained his own spiritual journey as a deeply personal search for elucidating his family secrets: presents of candied citrons his grandmother from Bastia sent every fall; strange old keys hidden in his grandparents' attic; their insistence on always living near the only synagogue on the island; many family traditions that he believed to be Corsican and which were, in fact, Jewish; and finally, his own professional interest—an over thirty-year-long scholarly fascination with Jesus, a Jewish man. "From a Jewish soul in a Christian body," said Long, "I therefore found mine."

Long explained that the island had "the Corsican Jewish memory, which is also mine and which is part of the Corsican soul." Long also stated that he knew of a number of Corsicans who became Orthodox Jews in Israel, perhaps just like him, by "awakening" of their Jewish souls. It was not coincidental then, summarized the journalist, that Corsica was the only region in France and, with the exception of Denmark, the only region in Europe that disobeyed the Nazis during the war and saved the Jews.

I was surprised to read that a former monk and a Christian scholar-turned-a-Jew, considered Judaism as not so much a religion but rather a great eternal tradition: "Moses received the Torah at Sinai and handed it over to Joshua; Joshua handed it over to the Elders; and the Elders handed it over to the Prophets…" According to Mr. Long, "Corsica knows this phenomenon of family oral tradition…and that tradition kept the Jewish soul alive in Corsica." Long concluded: "It is Corsica that makes Corsicans." (Excerpts are from Halioua, Naoemie, "Conversation with Didier Meir Long." *L'Arche*, June 23, 2016).

Judaism is Alive and Well in Today's Corsica

"Jewish friends, are you leaving Ile-de-France? Come to the island of Corsica: everyone will leave you alone."
Antoine Albertini, Editor-in-Chief, *Corse Matin*, on anti-Semitic violence in France as the reason for a growing number of French Jews deciding to emigrate. Jan. 16, 2018.

Corsican people are what truly set the island apart from the rest of the world, admitted Rabbi Levi Pinson to *Chabad Magazine* in the summer of 2018. "I never was exposed to demonstrations of anti-Semitism here (in Corsica), similar to what I encountered in, for example, France," the Rabbi confirmed during an interview for the article "A Journey to Chabad of Corsica." Rabbi Pinson added: "On the contrary, I constantly am met only with generosity and displays of admiration." (*Chabad Magazine*, August 20, 2018). It is only fitting for the island, where the current President of the Executive Council is Jewish.

At the conclusion of the interview, Rabbi Pinson pointed out that the head of the island's government, Gilles Simeoni, had a Jewish mother of Polish origin. Pinson also added that Simeoni was born on *Yud-Alef Nissan* or the eleventh day of the Jewish calendar month of Nissan, which is a birthday of the Chabad-venerated Rebbe Menachem Mendel Schneerson, a highly important fact for Orthodox Jews.

Young Rabbi Pinson arrived in Bastia from Nice at the end of 2016 with a goal of reviving Jewish life on the island. As a dedicated "Chabadnik," Rabbi Pinson stated that his mandate was to "restore the glory of Yiddishkait." Pinson, his wife Mushky Pinson, and other Chabad members who joined them did much more. By establishing Chabad headquarters in Ajaccio and branches in cities like Bastia, Porto-Vecchio, and some others, they started a full-blown revival of Jewish life on the island widely appreciated by not only Jews but also by the non-Jewish population of Corsica.

In December 2017, Rabbi Pinson lectured to the captive and mostly non-Jewish audience about the approaching Hanukkah holiday, its meaning, and symbols. The Rabbi described the tradition established in some big cities to light a giant menorah in the town's central square. The audience encouraged him to meet with the mayor of Ajaccio about that: "Why should we be deprived of that tradition?" The mayor was not only supportive but also very enthusiastic about making the Hanukkah candle lighting a public celebration and an annual tradition in Ajaccio.

Hanukkah 2019 in Ajaccio, Corsica. From left to right: Rabbi Levi Pinson, Mayor of Ajaccio Laurent Marcangeli, and the Chief Imam of Ajaccio. The Hanukkiah is lit on the square just a few yards away from where Napoleon was born. The photo is courtesy of Chabad Corsica.

The first Hanukkah in Corsica was celebrated in Ajaccio in December 2017. The event was organized by the Chabad as a worldwide Hanukkah celebration. This was how on an island where people were always averse to public religious displays,

Hanukkah celebrations in their capital Ajaccio have become an annual event. Accompanied by highly-spirited fanfare and publicity, these celebrations are attended by the Mayor of Ajaccio, Chief Imam of the local Muslim community, and hundreds of people of various religious and ethnic backgrounds. Is it a coincidence that the celebration takes place on Foch Square, just a stone throw away from Maison Bonaparte, the birthplace of Napoleon, the Champion of the Jews?

A growing number of people, who are re-discovering or becoming curious about their forgotten Jewish roots, come to Rabbi Pinson to learn more about Judaism and participate in Chabad programs. Likewise, the enrollment of children in Talmud Torah, a Jewish school, is growing: more children are coming to learn the Hebrew alphabet and basic concepts of Judaism.

To conclude my Corsican story, I want to return once again to Didier Meir Long, a theologian, a historian, a monk, a Jew, and a quintessential Corsican, who declared: "Judaism will be reborn in Corsica."

Hanukkah 2019. Ajaccio. In addition to Jews, all holiday celebrations organized by the Chabad attract hundreds of people from Christian and Muslim communities. The photo is courtesy of Chabad Corsica.

PART IV
A Field Guide to Jewish History Sites and Local Food in Corsica

As you already know after reading the previous part of this book, Corsicans are proud and fiercely independent people, who inhabit an island that was free from any foreign power for only fourteen years during its long history. Jewish history seekers will not find a Holocaust memorial or a Jewish heritage museum here. The Jewish narrative of Corsica still remains under the radar for most historians. Yet the island's Jewish history is over one thousand years old. And throughout these centuries, the people of Corsica, with their hearts always open to refugees escaping persecution and injustice, turned their island into a safe haven for many Jews.

Anywhere you go in Corsica, always remember when you see the Corsicans in those picturesque mountain villages and beautiful seaside towns, that their parents, or grandparents were unknown and unsung heroes during World War II. Thanks to the combined power of *Omerta* (the Mafia's code of silence) and the generous Corsican heart, many Corsicans risked their lives saving thousands of French Jews fleeing from Nazi-occupied mainland France. The only monument to Corsicans' bravery and generosity is the island itself.

This Field Guide is based on our detailed research and actual on-the-ground experience, both of which are reflected in Part III called Corsica—The Island of Beauty, the Island of the Just. Some of the information mentioned in Part III was also included in this Part IV for your convenience to better assist you during the visits to the locations. Below, we describe the sites, cities, and places related to the Corsican Jewish history. However, this book is by no means a comprehensive guide to the island, but rather a useful companion for a Corsica traveler interested in the history of the Jewish people who came to this island, be it centuries ago or in modern times.

Depending on your arrival airport and the towns you choose as a base, the order of the Jewish history places you decide to visit can be changed. The suggested base-cities, in no particular order, are: Bastia, Calvi, Ajaccio, and Bonifacio. As your day trips go, Corte, a must for any history buff, is an easy scenic drive from any of these cities. L'Île Rousse is very close to Calvi. Filitosa is located about halfway between Ajaccio and Bonifacio. A stop at the village of Levie could be combined with a visit to Porto-Vecchio for an enjoyable day trip from Bonifacio. The map that follows shows all the sites recommended in this guide. These are the towns and villages we consider highly important for understanding the Jewish story of Corsica in the context of the island itself, its people, and its history.

With no convenient public transportation on the island, your rental car, a detailed map, either a GPS app on your phone or a separate GPS, and this book are your essential tools. We suggest you reread the related chapters in this book prior to visiting the sites on our "Jewish History Path." Happy travels!

Right: Location of the recommended sites on the map of Corsica.

Visiting Filitosa: the Most Famous Prehistoric Site in Corsica

Why Visit Filitosa?

In Filitosa, a National Historic Monument Site, you begin your investigation into what made Corsicans ... well ... Corsicans. This is an important step in understanding the Jewish story of the island in the context of its history. In Filitosa, you enter the portal into a mysterious civilization of ancient Corsica and the people who created it.

The site consists of a museum and an adjacent park. In the museum, you learn about Corsicans' connection to the ancient rebellious tribes of Sherden warriors, possible ancestors of the islanders' fierce independent spirit. Walking through the park, you find yourself in a place like no other: surrounded by strange ruins of round stone houses, towers, and mysterious anthropomorphic statue-menhirs. Those are man-made upright standing stones, each with a different chiseled face, all armed with a sword-like weapon.

Even today, scientists do not agree on the origins of these mysterious figures and structures. Who were the creators of those enigmatic statues? What was their purpose: ceremonial, healing, or commemorating historical events? Were they erected by

Right: In Filitosa, the menhirs tightly guard their secrets.

The remains of the face on this menhir are rather sketchy. However, the shape of the sword is fairly realistic.

the Sherden warriors, the prehistoric forebears of these proud and independent-minded people you meet during your travels through the island?

While making your acquaintance with statue-menhirs in Filitosa, do not overlook the architectural evidence of prehistoric Corsican-

Top: The ruins of a round structure.

Right: Location of Filitosa on the map of Corsica.

Sardinian connections: ruins of round towers, called "torri" in Filitosa.

Where is Filitosa?

Filitosa is located in the southwest part of the island in the municipality of Sollacaro. If your initial base is Ajaccio and you are driving to Filitosa from this city, follow your navigation device south via T40 or D355. If you are staying in Bonifacio and will travel to Filitosa from there via route T40, we suggest you leave yourself at least an hour to stop in Sartene, a picturesque medieval town that a famous French writer Prosper Mérimée called "the most Corsican of all the Corsican towns." Sartene boasts a fine museum with an excellent prehistoric artifacts collection.

Address: Filitosa, D.57, 20140 Sollacaro.
The site information can be obtained from their website https://www.filitosa.fr/en/ or by calling +33 (0) 4 95 74 00 91.

Key Sites to Visit
The museum and the park.

Sartene, "the most Corsican of all the Corsican towns," is a nice stop on the way to Filitosa from Bonifacio.

Visiting Corte: the Cradle of Corsican Independence

Why Visit Corte?

No other place in Corsica offers such an in-depth understanding of this island and the mindset of its people. The city itself is a symbol of Corsica. This is where Corsica as a democratic republic was born in 1755. Though the Republic lived for only fourteen years, its influence over the spirit of the Corsican people and their sense of identity cannot be overstated. For Jewish history enthusiasts, this city also represents the beginnings of modern Jewish history in the island.

Where is Corte?
Corte lies on route N193 (T20), about eighty kilometers northeast from the capital city of Ajaccio.

Location of Corte on the map of Corsica.

Key Sites to Visit

The Lower Town
Place Paoli. Place Paoli is a large square with a monument to the man called the "Father of the Nation" in the center. The

establishment of the Republic in 1755 and that of the safe haven for the Jews in Corsica were in many respects possible due to a Corsican hero, Pascal Paoli (1725–1807).

Pascal Paoli led Corsicans in their fight against Genoa and France. He established an independent democratic state, wrote its Constitution, and founded the University of Corte, just to mention a few of his nation-building accomplishments. Paoli also adopted the Moor's Head that you see everywhere in Corsica, as a national emblem and a flag of the Corsican Republic.

Right: So much to see!

Place Paoli.

Statue of Pascal Paoli.

What you need to remember about Pascal Paoli and the Jews

The "Father of the Nation" to Corsicans, Pascal Paoli had also become "the Father" to the Jewish community of the Republic he created. He was an enlightened leader who firmly believed in human rights and political and social equality for all. "The Jews have the same rights as Corsicans, since they share the same fate," he proclaimed. During the fourteen years of the Republic, Paoli brought thousands of Jews to Corsica. See "The Jews of Paoli" in Part III of this book.

Place Gaffori. Going westward from Place Paoli, you come to Place Gaffori with a large statue at the center dedicated to another renowned hero of Corsican independence, Jean-Pierre Gaffori.

He led the major insurrection against the Genoese conquerors in 1745-1755 and took a large territory of the island from the Genoese before he was killed in an ambush in 1753.

Walking uphill from Place Paoli to Place Gaffori.

Circle the statue to see the base reliefs representing Gaffori's heroic accomplishments and find the relief dedicated to his brave wife Faustina. Read about her in the chapter devoted to Corte. Faustina deserves to be remembered!

Place Gaffori. The house of Jean-Pierre Gaffori is behind his statue.

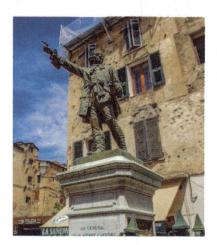

Look around the square. The house where the Gaffori family lived stands behind his statue, opposite one of the town's oldest buildings, the 15th-century church Eglise de l'Annonciation. Notice that the Gaffori house façade still shows holes from

Left: Frontal view of Gaffori statue and his house.

The Eglise de l'Annonciation church, 15th century, one of the town's oldest buildings.

bullets fired in 1746 during the Italians' fight against the Corsican rebels.

The Fountain of the Four Cannons. Close to Gaffori square, on the Commandant Ignace Mantel's Ramp, find an unusual fountain called the Fountain of the Four Cannons.

This medieval-looking, pyramid-shaped structure was actually built at the end of the eighteenth century, in 1778, when the

Republic had been dead for nine years, and Corsica was officially part of France. The French King Louis XVI commissioned the fountain to channel water from the mountain torrents to the local garrison stationed in Corte to deal with those troublesome Corsicans.

The Fountain of the Four Cannons.

The Upper Town

Head toward the Upper Town and the Citadel built by the Genoese in 1419.

Palais National. Before reaching the entrance to the bastions of the Citadel, stop on the Place du Poilu to visit the Palais National. Built in the seventeenth century, this building was a residence of the Genoese governors of Corsica.

The doorway to the Palais National on Place du Poilu.

When the Republic was proclaimed, the mansion became the residence of the young nation's President, Pascal Paoli. Corsican independence was declared here. The birthplace of the sovereign state, Palais National served as a seat of the new Corsican parliament for 14 years. Now, fittingly enough, the building houses the Institute of Corsican Studies.

Casanova House where Napoleon's older brother Joseph was born.

The Casanova House. While contemplating the short-lived Corsican republic, and staying in front of the Palais National, you might want to come closer to the orange building on the left. Called the Casanova House, this old mansion has an interesting historic connection, which leads to our home country, the United States.

Napoleon's older brother Joseph was born in Casanova House in 1768. Napoleon would appoint Joseph the Minister of Plenipotentiary and order him to negotiate a peace treaty with the United States in 1800. Joseph then briefly served as the King of Spain and Naples. For those of our readers who live in New Jersey, Joseph comes very close to home, literally: after Napoleon's downfall, Joseph immigrated to America and settled in Bordentown, New Jersey. And his estate will soon become a state park!

The Citadel. Now proceed to enter the Citadel, which had become a symbol of the islanders' fight for independence, especially when Pascal Paoli established the first Corsican University there. The Citadel houses the Musee de la Corse, the best historical museum on the island and a must for any history aficionado.

Entering the Citadel.

Walking along the ramparts of the Citadel.

View of Corte from the ramparts of the Citadel.

The top bastion of the Citadel.

Visiting Porto-Vecchio and the Levie Village: the Early Jewish Communities in Corsica

The history of the Jews in Corsica goes back at least a millennium. Around the year 800 CE, a large group of Jewish families arrived from Egypt in what is Porto-Vecchio today. They did not settle in Porto-Vecchio but went up into the mountains to build their new lives in a village that the locals would later name Levie. There are documents written in Hebrew kept in some ancient village churches in that mountainous region. Those Egyptian Jewish immigrants intermarried with the locals, assimilated, and disappeared into the island.

Where is Levie village?

The village of Levie exists today, and is located inland, approximately 40 kilometers from Porto-Vecchio and 58 kilometers from Bonifacio. If you are staying in Bonifacio, then driving from there to Levie takes a little more than an hour. If you are driving to Levie from Porto-Vecchio, the trip should take about an hour. For more information on the village and the Jews who came there, see "The Early Jewish Communities" in Part III of this book.

Why Visit Porto-Vecchio and Levie Village?

Staying in Bonifacio, you would be conveniently located for a greatly enjoyable day trip visiting both Porto-Vecchio and Levie. In Porto-Vecchio, enjoy the beautiful marina and take advantage of the gorgeous beaches. In the mountain village still called Levie, you will be bound to feel its romantic charm. But no Jews live there today and have not for centuries.

So, why go there? Indeed, reconstructing Corsican Jewish history is like trying to read an ancient manuscript where some pages are greatly damaged by time and some are missing completely. What firmly comes across, however, is the welcoming Corsican heart, always open to those who seek refuge from persecution and injustice. Put your imagination in high gear and think about those Jewish families from Egypt, rejoicing at the site of Porto-Vecchio as an entrance to safety and later, moving inland, away from the coast to safer places in the mountains.

Locations of Porto-Vecchio and Levie on the map of Corsica.

Visiting L'Île Rousse: the Jews of Paoli

Why Visit L'Île Rousse?

L'Île Rousse, a commune in the northwestern part of Corsica, was founded by Pascal Paoli in 1758 in order for the Republic to have a port that was not ruled by the Genoese, who, at that time, still controlled some ports on the island. This is where the modern Jewish history of Corsica had its beginnings. Paoli, the leader of the new Republic of Corsica, invited Jewish merchants and entrepreneurs from Italy and Spain to settle in L'Île Rousse. Later, those newcomers were even called "the Jews of Paoli." The Corsican leader clearly understood that the young nation, after being exploited by the Genoese for five hundred years, needed to build a firm economic foundation. This is where Jewish merchants were indispensable.

L'Île Rousse is located by a beautiful bay with white sand beaches and reddish-colored stone islets. It has recently become a Riviera-style resort. Most tourist brochures mention that the red islets around L'Île Rousse are the reason for the town's name. However, I came across some sources stating that the town got its name from ... the Jews! Most of these immigrants' names were hard to pronounce for the locals, and they nicknamed the new arrivals, some of whom had red hair, *Rossu*, which means a "redhead" or plural *Rossi*. While "the Jews of Paoli" had also assimilated and "disappeared" into Corsica, the surname Rossi remains widespread among the Corsicans.

Where is L'Île Rousse?

L'Île Rousse is only 24 kilometers from Calvi, which is now one of the most popular vacation destinations on the island due to its beautiful marina and overall natural magnificence. From Calvi to L'Île Rousse is less than a 30-minute drive. We included a couple of photos from Calvi hoping to entice you to spend some time in this beatiful city.

Right: Locations of L'Île Rousse on the map of Corsica.

Calvi marina.

Walking along the Calvi marina towards the bastion.

Visiting Ajaccio: Napoleon and the Jews

Why Visit Ajaccio?

The capital of Corsica has an unmistakable imperial look and should be a must destination for any history enthusiast. This is where Napoleon Bonaparte was born (1769) and raised. In Jewish history, Napoleon is one of the greatest heroes. Napoleon's Civil Code of 1804 granted religious freedom to all people, including the Jews. During the Napoleonic Wars (1804-1815), Bonaparte spearheaded the emancipation of the Jews of Western Europe outlawing ghettoization. In Ajaccio, one meets Napoleon everywhere.

Location of Ajaccio on the map of Corsica.

Key Sites to Visit

Walk along the Cours Napoleon, the main boulevard that crosses the entire city and is frequently intersected by small alleys leading down to the sea or up to the hills.

Maison Bonaparte. On Rue Saint-Charles, you find the Maison Bonaparte, the house where Ajaccio's hero was born, now a museum that displays a couch where Napoleon's mother gave birth to him.

Maison Bonaparte is located on Rue Saint-Charles.

Entrance to the Maison Bonaparte, the Bonaparte family mansion.

Place de Gaulle. Next, stop at the Place de Gaulle that is dominated by the monument to Napoleon on horseback dressed like a Roman

Monument to Napoleon on Place de Gaulle.

Emperor and surrounded by his four brothers in Roman senatorial togas. A great place to take a breather and reminisce about some unexpected historical curiosities bringing you to the …. United States. In Corte, you have already learned about Joseph and his New Jersey connection.

However, it was the Bonaparte's youngest brother Jerome's grandson who provided the strongest U.S. connection. Charles Joseph Bonaparte served as the United States Secretary of the Navy and the United States Attorney General in President Theodore Roosevelt's administration, 1901-1909. In 1908, Charles Joseph established a Bureau of Investigation that grew under J. Edgar Hoover to become the modern-day F.B.I.

Place d'Austerlitz. Now, look for the street running parallel to the sea, Cours Gandval, which will take you to the Place d'Austerlitz. You might like to walk for about 1.5 km and enjoy the view or choose to conserve your energy and take a lovely tiny train, like the one in the photo, instead.

Cours Gandval runs parallel to the sea. It is an enjoyable but rather long walk that brings you to Place d'Austerlitz.

Instead of a long walk under the sun, you might prefer taking this miniature train that brings you to all Napoleon's landmarks.

Place d'Austerlitz with the monument called U Casone that commemorates Napoleon's victories.

U Casone monument to Napoleon.

An imposing monument called U Casone commemorates Napoleon's victories. His statue on the top of the hill dominates the square. The emperor wears his renowned two-cornered hat. This is a copy of the famous statue placed in front of Napoleon's memorial in Les Invalides in Paris.

Palais Fesch. There is one more place in Ajaccio that we consider of high importance for all history aficionados, whether they seek places associated with Napoleon or are in search of a Jewish story: Palais Fesch, Musee des Beaux-Arts of Ajaccio. The Palais Fesch was built by Napoleon's uncle

Musee des Beaux-Arts of Ajaccio is located in the Palais Fesch.

Cardinal Joseph Fesch (1763-1839). As a highly knowledgeable collector, he dedicated three of the building's wings to house his extensive art collection. I know, I know, you are in Corsica after all, and you might want to take a break from the endless succession of art museums you visited in Europe… However, for the Jewish history seeker, here is an interesting detail about Joseph Fesch, Napoleon's uncle.

The uncle was close to Napoleon and supported his political and military career. However, the cardinal strongly objected to Bonaparte's policy related to Jews. A Napoleonic scholar Dr. Ben Weider writes that the Joseph Fesch told Napoleon: "Do you know the Holy Scriptures predict the end of the world when the Jews are recognized as belonging to a Christian Nation as equals?" The Cardinal even refused to participate in the coronation ceremony when Napoleon became the emperor, saying: "Sire, you wish the end of the world to come with you giving the Jews equality…"

Ajaccio port. The Jewish refugees from the Middle East arrived there in 1915-1920.

It is only fitting for the contemporary Corsican Jewish story to begin in the city that gave the world one of the most passionate champions of the Jews.

Finding the Jewish Story in Ajaccio

Gare Maritime. Go to the Gare Maritime on Quai L'Herminier, which is only a few-minutes walk north of the main tourist office on Place Foch, Ajaccio's main square. This port was the entrance to a new safe life for the twentieth-century Jewish refugees from in the Middle East during World War I.

They were mostly the Jewish families from the French mandated countries, like Syria and Lebanon. Imagine those desperate people disembarking from a French military boat in Ajaccio.

In December of 1915, the French government allowed a number of Jewish families, mostly from Syria and Lebanon, to come to France. However, they were not admitted to the mainland, but instead, sent to Corsica, the island of poverty and misery. Navy ships took the immigrants to Ajaccio.

As it happened before, Corsicans, despite their own deprivations, full heartedly welcomed the refugees who were not allowed by the Ottomans to take with them any savings or possessions. The local population shared their meager resources to help the newcomers start a new life in Corsica. The unoccupied Catholic seminary was quickly remodeled to provide each family with a separate dormitory room, an auditorium was transformed into a synagogue, a *mikveh* (a ritual bath) was installed, and even (somewhat) kosher food was provided.

At that time, a small Jewish community had already been living in Bastia. So, sometime after arriving in Ajaccio, some Jews, mostly Moroccan families, left for Bastia. Many other families followed later.

While looking for that Seminary building in Ajaccio, we were told that the old structure was demolished in 1968.

Chabad Corsica. But before going to the north of the island to Bastia, where the only synagogue in Corsica is located, you might want to stop by one more place in Ajaccio that symbolizes the rebirth of Judaism in Corsica in the 21st century: Chabad Corsica-Ajaccio.

In preparation for your trip, you might want to call the Ajaccio Chabad headquarters office at 33-7-55-2737-6 and speak with Rabbi Levi Pinson, Director, or his wife, Mrs. Mushky Pinson, Co-Director. Another option is to send an email to either one of them from the Chabad Corsica website: https://www.chabad.org/centers/default_cdo/aid/3409050/jewish/Chabad-of-Corsica.htm. The Ajaccio office and the kosher grocery store, Beth Chabad, are located on Rue de Vittolo.

If the Rabbi or his wife is able to meet with you, you will hear a fascinating story of their arrival in Corsica in 2016 and their successful work. You will learn about a full-blown revival of Jewish life on the island, widely appreciated not only by the Jews but also by the non-Jewish population of Corsica. Ask them specifically about their famous annual all-town Hanukkah celebration often attended by hundreds of people.

Visiting Bastia: Home of the Only Synagogue in Corsica

Why Visit Bastia?

Bastia is the second largest city in Corsica after Ajaccio. It is the island's military headquarters and its economic capital. Spend some time at the fine museum of Bastia history, Musee de Bastia, located in the elegant Palais des Gouverneurs, which used to house the Genoese governors. The palace is located in the upper ("new") town (Terra Nuova). Bastia citadel that looms over the harbor is a fine example of mediaeval fortifications.

From the Jewish history perspective, the city of Bastia is the city where the refugees during World War I came after their short stop in Ajaccio. Bastia is the only Corsican city that has a synagogue.

Where is Bastia?

Located on the northeastern coast, Bastia is one of the busiest French ports in the Mediterranean.

Key Site to Visit

Synagogue Beth Meir. In 1934, the synagogue Beth Meir was founded in an apartment, located at the number 3 Rue de Castagno, in the historic part of the city. If you plan a visit, we suggest you try calling the synagogue in advance at 33-6-10-2729-12 to find out about the best time to tour the synagogue. Keep in mind that, whoever answers the phone, most likely does not speak English.

Today, with the exception of the Chabad centers, Beth Meir is the only synagogue in Corsica. Its name, Beth Knesset Beth Meir, was chosen as a tribute to Rabbi Meir, a philosopher mentioned in the Mishnah. The diminishing community consists of a few elderly families, and the services are held only on Shabbat and during the holidays. Why didn't these few remaining Jews of Corsica leave the island? The answer given by an elderly lady was: "In what location in the world were Jews more welcome than in Corsica?"

The entrance door of the Synagogue Beth Meir. Reprinted with permission from the ANU Museum of the Jewish People, The Oster Visual Documentation Center. Courtesy of Louis Davidson, Synagogues 360.

Inside the Synagogue Beth Meir. Reprinted with permission from the ANU Museum of the Jewish People, The Oster Visual Documentation Center. Courtesy of Louis Davidson, Synagogues 360.

Right: Location of Bastia on the map of Corsica.

Exploring Culinary Treasures of Corsica

Corsican food tells the story of the island and its people. Though often unique, it reflects many influences of the conquerors who controlled the island throughout the centuries. For example, the Greeks brought in olives in the third century BCE, and the Genoese introduced chestnuts in the sixteenth century. At the same time, Corsica's mountainous terrain, rugged coastline, and its climate also shaped their great produce, herbs, and typical food staples that every Corsican is greatly proud of.

Observing Kosher in Corsica

For the observant Jewish globe-trotters, Chabad Corsica is the best source of information on kosher restaurants and JOFY (Jewish Observant Friendly) establishments on the island.

An old café in Bonifacio.

In preparation for your trip, you can call the Ajaccio Chabad headquarters office at 33-7-55-2737-6 and speak with Rabbi Levi Pinson, Director, or his wife, Mrs. Mushky Pinson, Co-Director. Another option is to send an email to either one of them from the Chabad Corsica website. The Ajaccio office and the kosher grocery store, Beth Chabad, are located on Rue de Vittolo.

Additionally, a well-known source of kosher-related travel information globally is TotallyJewishTravel.com.

Definitely Not Kosher—But—Do Not Leave Corsica without Trying Some of Their Specialties!

The *Charcuterie* (a plate of smoked meats) is the pride of the island and an absolute must to try for a non-vegetarian, non-vegan, and not kosher-observant traveler. Since both Alex and I are neither vegetarians nor kashrut-observant, we would often supper on smoked meats, cheeses, crusty bread, and local rosé wine—all bought in small shops in Calvi, Bonifacio, and Ajaccio.

The Corsicans we talked to in the stores would gladly explain that their pigs, of which there are over 45,000 on the island, are semi-wild, live in the woods, and feed on chestnuts, acorns, and wild herbs. What they eat contributes to the Corsican meats' unique flavors. Even though pork is almost never on our menu at home, we simply had to try the local delicacies to round up our exploration of Corsica. We loved Corsican meats: *prisuttu* (cured ham), *lonzu* (smoked beef or pork fillet), and *figatellu* (smoked sausage). Locals believe that their smoked meats, especially *prisuttu*, are best when carved by hand.

But what I still miss most are the cheeses. We enjoyed Corsican cheeses with a bit of their local fig or apricot jam. The *niolo* is a variety of rather strong aged cheese, which, perhaps, is not to everyone's taste. As for us—we loved it! One English-speaking storeowner told us that all their cheeses were filled with flavors of Corsican mountains, where ewes (sheep) graze on unfertilized pastures covered with wild herbs. In addition, the way cheeses were made had not changed much over the centuries, he added. We were told that the *brocciu* cheese, the Corsican claim to fame, was made from heated ewe's milk, similar to Italian-style ricotta, and whey. Plain *brocciu* is often blended with local mint and used in their popular dish—stuffed baked aubergine (small eggplant).

The main dishes in Corsica are often meat, meat, and meat. Sorry again, vegetarians and vegans. The veal and olive stew is a classic. Corsican cattle graze in the maquis, dense ever-green bushes with fragrant yellow flowers that cover, I read, well over forty percent of the island. They are invasive and prickly, and for Corsicans the maquis is the symbol of their land. ("I can always recognize my island by the smell of the maquis," said Napoleon). Locals believe that their veal dishes are so good because of the maquis pastures.

I, however, preferred Corsican seafood; after all, Corsica is an island! Their sardines are really good, as well as bass, swordfish, and mullet. My favorite was crispy fried red mullet (also called goatfish) stuffed with anchovies.

As we learned, the Corsicans consider a true Corsican meal what they call *a minestra*. This dish, as you can guess, is a soup, a vegetable soup to be exact. The *minestra* is usually cooked with beans and always with all kind of vegetables a housewife has at home. Someone explained to us that there are as many *minestra* recipes as there are villages and towns on the island.

Chestnuts are as ubiquitous to Corsica as the Moor's Head emblem. They are a beloved legacy of the hated Genoese conquerors who planted chestnut plantations, or rather forests, all over the island. Chestnut flower honey is strong and has a somewhat exotic taste that we liked very much. Corsicans use dried chestnuts to make flour, which is an essential ingredient in many local dishes. I especially liked chestnut flour cookies and the Beignets, a Corsican beloved dessert that looks like our doughnut, though it is anything but. The Beignets are shaped like rings and deep-fried, but the similarities end there. This dessert is often made with *brocciu* cheese, which gives it a unique and delicious flavor!

And of course, Corsican wines should not be overlooked. Most Corsican wines are made in what is called AOC zones, like Cap Corse, Calvi, Sartene, Porte-Vecchio, and others.

Enjoying Corsican seafood with their crusty bread in Bonifacio.

Corsican white wines are very popular but we preferred the rosé wines like *Patrimonio* and Vins de Corse.

Most reds are full-bodied and have rich flavor. I liked *Clos Alivu Patrimonio*: it was very dry and had a slight taste of wild herbs.

Back home, I was able to find and order it online, along with a Corsican Rose bottle. I wish I had as much luck with Corsican cheeses…

Disclaimer: All addresses and contact information were accurate as of the time of writing.

My first Corsican meal in Ajaccio is *a minestra*!

Select Movies Filmed in Corsica

Before any trip, Alex and I love to watch a few movies filmed on location in places we are about to visit. We often watch some of them again after we return, if for nothing else but a joyous yelp of recognition from the two of us at the same time: "We were there! Remember?!"

Below are a few films we liked, some for the artistic and cinematographic aspects, some for the beautiful scenery, and some for both. This is not, by any means, a comprehensive list, but rather a sample of movies we enjoyed and the places in Corsica that now exist forever in our own mental landscape. The order is chronological and spans the time period from 1962 to 2017.

1962 – *The Longest Day*. Directors: Darryl Zanuck, Ken Anakin, Bernard Wicki, and others.
This film is about the D-Day and Allies' landing in Normandy. The location: near Bastia, beaches of Saint Florent. The international cast included Richard Burton, Sean Connery, Henry Fonda, and John Wayne.

1997 – *Hikers* (*Les Randonneurs*). Director: Philippe Harel. A comedy about a group of Parisians walking along a famous Corsican hiking trail called GR20. The locations include Ajaccio, Calvi, and Corte.

2004 – *A Very Long Engagement* (*Un Long Dimanche de Fiancailles*). Director: Jean-Pierre Jeunet. A love story staring Audrey Tautou and Marion Cotilard. Some scenes are filmed in Calvi.

2004 – *The Corsican File* (*L'Enquete Corse*). Director: Alan Berberian. A private investigator is looking for a man who has inherited a property. The locations: Ajaccio, L'Île Rousse, and Sartene.

2017 – *A Violent Life (Une Vie Violente)*. Director: Thierry de Peretti. A Corsican man returns to his hometown in Corsica for the funeral of his friend and re-discovers a violent world he tried to leave behind. Some scenes shot in Bastia and environs.

About the Author

For Irene Shaland, globe-trotting is a passion and a way of life. She sees travel as a process of personal growth and an opportunity to share her knowledge and experiences with her readers who are also enthusiastic about history, arts, and legends from the four corners of the earth. Irene and Alex, her husband and an award-winning travel photographer, have visited close to 80 countries and enchanted audiences with their books, magazine articles, lectures, and photography exhibits based on their travels.

Irene Shaland is an internationally published art and travel writer, Jewish historian, and educator. In her research, publications, and lectures she focuses on the rich tapestry of global Jewish experiences, culture, and heritage. Her third book *The Dao of Being Jewish and Other Stories* was released in 2016. Irene's close to thirty articles are published in the U.S., Canada, U.K., France, South Africa, and Israel. A sought-after presenter, Irene lectures extensively nationally and internationally at conferences, museums, research centers, synagogues, Jewish Federations, art galleries, and societies. She is the President of the GTA Books publishing company and a founding member of the Global Travel Authors Group.

About the Photographer

Alex Shaland, the author of "Suburbanites on Safari," is an internationally-published photographer. Alex's photographs appeared in various journals and other media in the U.S., Canada, France, Kenya, South Korea, and the U.K.

Website: https://globaltravelauthors.com
Twitter: @ShalandGTA
Facebook: https://www.facebook.com/GlobalTravelAuthors

Made in the USA
Las Vegas, NV
15 July 2022